· THE ·
VAIL HIKER
· And Ski Touring Guide ·

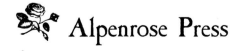

Alpenrose Press

Try These 10 New Trails

· THE ·
VAIL HIKER
· And Ski Touring Guide ·

50 Historic Hiking, Snowshoe and Ski Trails in Eagle County, the Holy Cross and Gore Range Wilderness Areas

by Mary Ellen Gilliland

Library of Congress Catalog Card Number: 96-84848

ISBN: 1-889385-06-9

Fourth edition, revised, 2004

Back cover photo courtesy Colorado State Historical Society
Ten of this book's maps are printed from TOPO!, copyright 2001 National Geographic Holdings (www.topo.com)

Visit Our New Web Site! **www.alpenrosepress.com** for weekly featured trails, hiking, ski and high altitude tips and more!

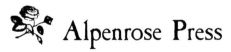
Alpenrose Press
Box 499
Silverthorne, Colorado 80498
(970) 468-6273
orders@alpenrosepress.com

CONTENTS

SPECIAL HIKES FOR KIDS

Hikers today remain intrigued by the storied Mount of the Holy Cross just as nine-teenth-century America thrilled to its "discovery" by photographer William Henry Jackson in 1873.

Snow from the. Mount of the Holy Cross melts to fill the Bowl of Tears, a lake deep in the raw rock ravine below the mount. Early pilgrims also saw the supplicant figure of a woman in the snowfield right of the cross. Colorado Historical Society photo.

TRAILS BY DIFFICULTY

SKI/SNOWSHOE TOURS BY DIFFICULTY

Fresh air, fresh snow and a faithful friend are all a snowshoer really needs. Brad Odekirk Photo

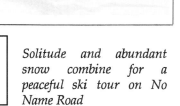

Solitude and abundant snow combine for a peaceful ski tour on No Name Road

Echoes of boom towns, and ghost towns, from the area's past still resonate.

THE

VAIL HIKER
· And Ski Touring Guide ·

TRAIL MAP

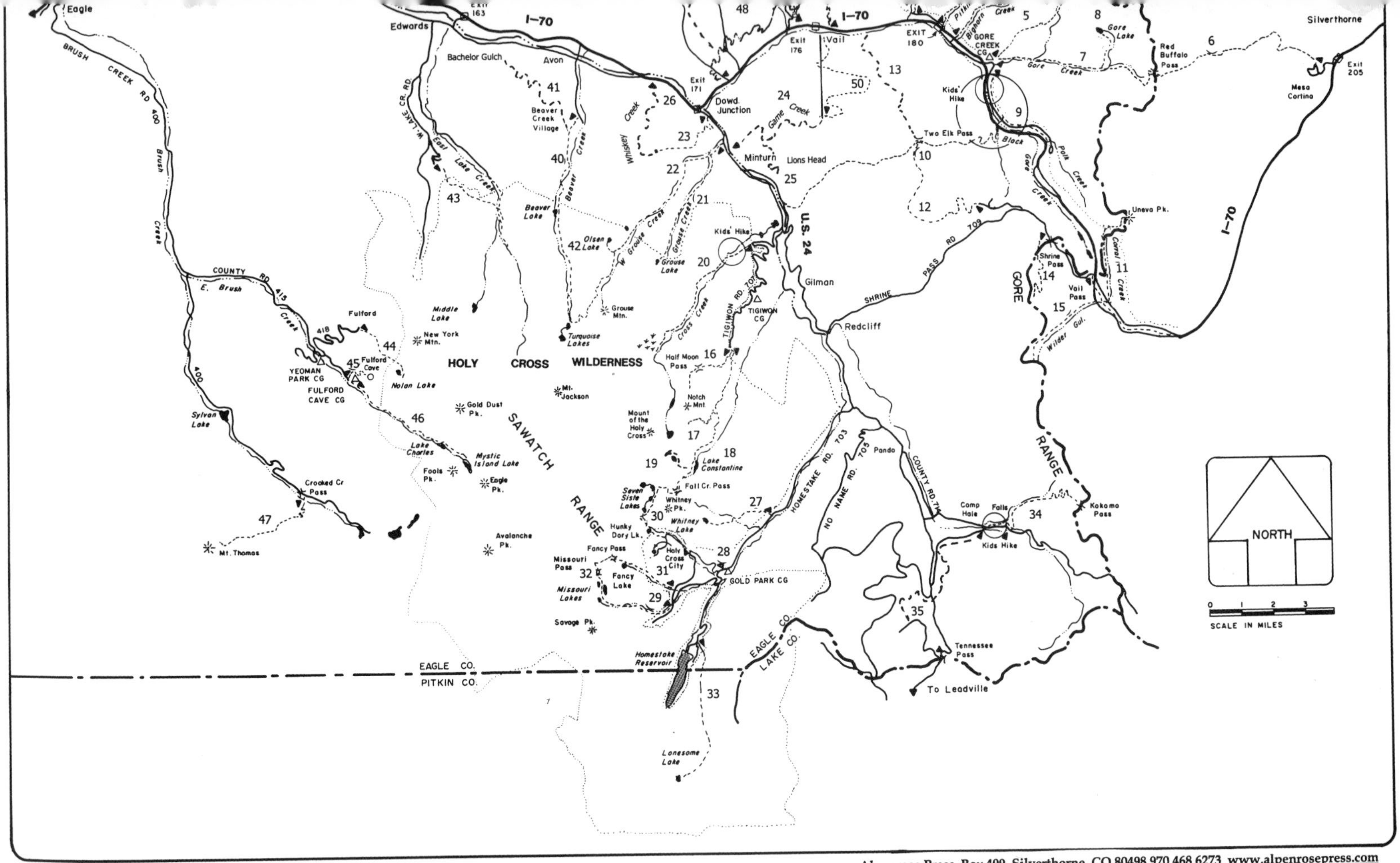

NORTH

SCALE IN MILES
0 1 2 3

Alpenrose Press, Box 499, Silverthorne, CO 80498 970 468 6273 www.alpenrosepress.com

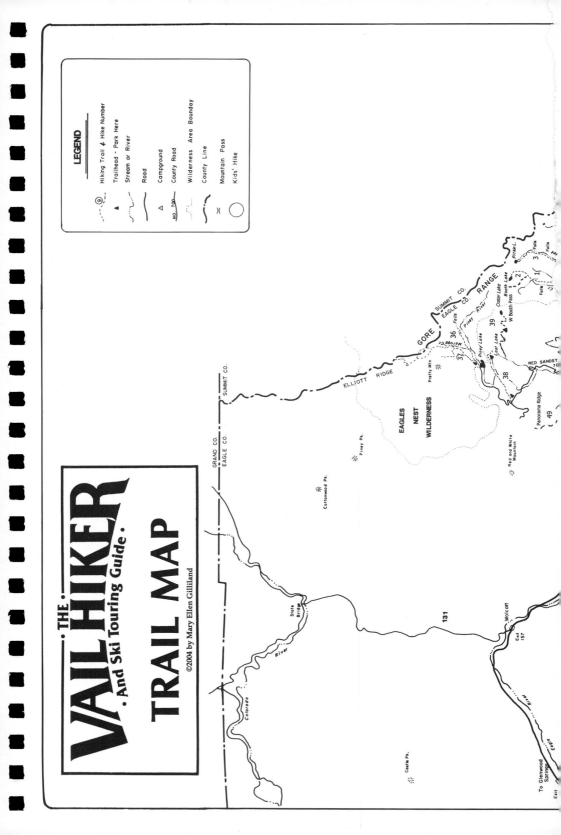

·THE· VAIL HIKER
·And Ski Touring Guide·
©2004 by Mary Ellen Gilliland
TRAIL MAP

LEGEND

⑨	Hiking Trail & Hike Number
▲	Trailhead - Park Here
〰	Stream or River
〜	Road
△	Campground
NO. 700	County Road
〜	Wilderness Area Boundary
—··—	County Line
)(	Mountain Pass
○	Kids' Hike

Trail of the Week!

New every Monday on our web site:

Author Mary Ellen Gilliland selects
The Trail of the Week

The week's best
flowers
wildlife,
views
and trail conditions
at
www.alpenrosepress.com

Find Also

Hiking Guides
THE NEW SUMMIT HIKER

THE VAIL HIKER

Historical Books
**SUMMIT, A Gold Rush History
of Summit County, Colorado**

BRECKENRIDGE!
A Guide to the Ghost Towns

ACKNOWLEDGMENTS

Generous people lent time, enthusiasm and expertise to help launch THE VAIL HIKER. A warm thank you goes to Jim Guest, U.S. Forest Service trails expert with the Holy Cross Ranger District office at Minturn, who counseled on the original edition, then shared his working trails knowledge to critique the manuscript.

Special thanks to Bill Johnson, Eagle Ranger District, who advised on trails near East Lake Creek and Old Fulford. Rick Jewell, Recreation forester in Minturn, offered guidance and manuscript evaluation.

Dave Morgan, Vail Associates, spent time brainstorming trail ideas and gave us a day with Vail mountain guide, Ingrid Gianetti. Jean Naumann, Beaver Creek cross country center manager, shared her enthusiasm for skiing at Beaver Creek's McCoy Park. Vail author-historian June Simonton steered us to rich stores of Eagle County historical treasure.

Getting the manuscript into book form required the help of big-hearted folks: Robin and Patty Theobald, along with John Farr, shared computer equipment. Copy editors Jack and Elsa Gilliland, cover artist Mike Keefe and graphic designer Danette Peterson lent time and talent. Sheliah Gilliland volunteered as proofreader.

Revising the book for its 1996 edition also required kind people's help. A warm thank you goes to Holy Cross Ranger District trails specialist Beth Boyst. The Eagle Ranger District's Bill Johnson advised once again. Hiking trails guide Juli Young generously lent her expertise. Town of Vail senior environmental planner Russell Forest gave a valuable assist on plans for North Vail Trail.

For the 2001 edition the Holy Cross Ranger District's trail specialist, Steve Bull, consulted. In 2004, Trails Supervisor Don Dressler gave valuable assistance. Bill Johnson again checked facts. Hiker Janie Saul advised in 2004 and Tom Yacono helped with typography.

Warmest thanks to Larry Gilliland, trail-finder, business manager, computer wizard whose computer creativity made each edition possible.

M.E.G.

PLEASE READ THIS BEFORE HIKING

BEFORE YOU BEGIN...

In the beginning, God created the heavens and the earth. (Genesis 1:1)

The splendor of creation shines forth in snow-capped peaks that scrape the sky, flower-dappled alpine meadows, dark forest cut by crystal streams. Eagle County abounds in nature's beauty and offers a variety of terrain, from fluttering aspen forest through evergreen wood to sun-swept open tundra. Relics from its gold rush and homestead ranching days remain to intrigue Vail-area hikers.

Fifty hikes into the pristine Gore Range and Holy Cross Wilderness areas, plus the White River National Forest, are highlighted. There are eight hikes into the spectacular Gore Range Wilderness above East Vail; seven on Vail Pass; eight trails into the awe-inspiring Mount of the Holy Cross area near Minturn; eight Holy Cross Wilderness hikes around Homestake Reservoir; four trails near scenic Piney Lake; eight hikes west of Vail from Avon to Eagle's mountainous "back yard;" a route for gondola-tripping hikers on the Vail ski mountain; and two vista trails above Vail.

This guide seeks to help hikers avoid getting lost; to provide new trails for both local and visiting hikers to enjoy; to suggest mountain experiences for all levels of hikers from aggressive to recreational to families with first-time hikers. The author, Mary Ellen Gilliland, is a popular Colorado historian. (See *SUMMIT, A Gold Rush History of Summit County, Colorado* and *The New Summit Hiker & Ski Touring Guide*, Alpenrose Press, 970 468 6273.) She weaves an intriguing thread of the area's colorful history into each trail's description.

Each hike has an interesting destination, including waterfalls, lakes, early-day homestead cabins, passes, peaks, historic sites and view spots. Trails vary in length, from almost 16 miles to just one-half mile. They also vary in elevation. The Notch Mountain climb, which puts hikers face-to-face with the Mount of the Holy Cross, reaches a dizzying 13,100 feet. The short-but-sweet Fulford Cave walk rises to a milder 9,900 foot elevation.

HOW TO USE THE TRAIL STATISTICS:

Each trail chapter begins with seven facts that describe the hike: Time, distance, elevation gain, high point, rating, season open and topographic map required. Following are explanations for each.

Time: Times estimated refer to a round-trip hike and reflect a walking pace of 2 miles per hour. Time given includes rest stops, lunch break and brief exploring jaunts. Each hike's time is modified by trail difficulty and steepness. Individual hikers will set individual paces. The hour figure provides a general goal for hikers to inform family or friends of return time. Hours spent driving to and from the trailhead are not included.

Distance: Mileage is given for one-way only. Sometimes this guide's mileages and on-site trail signs will differ but usually in no significant way. Distance figures come from trail research, U.S. Forest Service figures and topographic map measurements.

Elevation gain: This number gives hikers a base to gauge the trail's difficulty. (Loss is not calculated.) However, hikers must consider gain together with distance. Example: The stiff trek up Fancy Pass climbs more than 800 feet from below Fancy Lake to the pass summit in 0.5 miles, while the Bowman's Shortcut trail gains the same 800 feet in 4 miles, a less demanding walk.

High point: The peak elevation describes the terrain hikers will reach. A lake at 9,800 feet will nestle in green pine forest while a tarn at 11,800 feet may pool below a granite headwall approached by flowery alpine meadows. For visitors from lower elevations, the trail's high point provides a guide for getting acclimated: Begin with Meadow Mountain (the entire climb stays below 10,000 feet) and work up.

Rating: Many hiking guides shirk trail rating because individuals evaluate trails in different ways. But most hikers need guidance on the ease or difficulty of the terrain. The rating, though subjective, is therefore included. Criteria for ratings included steepness, trail obstacles or hazards and difficulty in following the path.

Usually open: Snowmelt at extreme altitudes sometimes occurs as late as early July. Alpine lakes like Deluge sometimes (not always) remain frozen until July 4 and freeze again in September. Many local back country roads close in May and early June due to soggy spring run-off conditions. However, some trails, like lower-elevation and south-facing Whitney Lake and the North Vail Trail, open in mid-June. Elk calving closes Two Elk Trail till July 1.

Topo map: Topographic maps, a "must" for many of this book's hikes, are available from the U.S. Geological Survey's Central Region Map Distribution Center, Building 810, Denver Federal Center (Box 25286), Denver, Colorado 80225. Or, www.usgs.org/1-888-275-8747. Vail area sporting goods, mountaineering and backpacking stores also carry a complete map supply, along with clothing and gear for hikers, snowshoers and cross-country skiers.

To read a topographic map, study the contour lines, which connect points of equal elevation, distanced from sea level. The space between the contour lines, called the contour interval, measures vertical distance. When contour lines crowd close on the map, this indicates steepness. Spaced contour lines evidence more gentle terrain. You can calculate the interval on any topographic map by finding the difference between any two consecutive figures appearing along every fifth contour line and then dividing the figures by five. Check your map: Some use 20 foot intervals, while others use 200 foot intervals. Most of the book's topographic maps use a 40-foot interval. Always carry a map and compass; know how to use both.

The USGS maps have not kept pace with the Vail area boom. Map features such as towns fail to detail growth. And trail changes, such as the re-routing of the East Lake Creek Trail, do not show at present on available maps. Where these changes or omissions affect the hiker, the chapter text will underscore that fact.

Gray areas on our maps indicate vegetation while white shows above-timberline or open areas. If you don't wish to carry USGS topo maps, purchase the widely-available Trails Illustrated maps, which cover large areas and are photo-reduced from USGS maps.

YOUR RUCKSACK:

Map and **compass**—and the ability to use them—are essential. Eagle County's high altitude allows ultraviolet rays to penetrate clear air, so **sunglasses** are vital, as is **sunscreen** and possibly a long-sleeved shirt. **Insect repellent** comes in handy. Extra **shoes** and **socks** earn their keep for fording streams. Waterproof kitchen **matches** and a pocket **knife** serve many emergency uses, as do a **first aid kit** and **flashlight**. For summer storms, tote a water repellent **jacket or poncho**. For high altitude hikes, especially after September 1, carry a wool **hat** and **gloves, sweater** and **wind breaker** and a **down vest**. Don't forget high-energy **snacks** like hard candy, chocolate, dried fruit. Bring plenty of **water**. Finally: Always carry a **litter bag**.

THE WILDERNESS AREAS:

Eagles Nest: Eleven of this guide's hikes penetrate the 133,496-acre Eagles

Nest Wilderness, a primitive area in the Gore Range. Its jagged peaks pierce the sky and its mountains are arranged in a wild jumble.

Holy Cross: Eighteen of *The Vail Hiker* trails wind through the Holy Cross Wilderness, a rugged and beautiful region dominated by the soaring Sawatch Range. Over 100 miles of constructed trails crisscross the Holy Cross' 123,410 acres. One-third of the primitive area is above timberline, with the Continental Divide forming its southern boundary.

Wilderness Rules: Mountain bikes are not permitted in the wilderness and dogs must be on a 6-foot or shorter leash. Groups are limited to 12; campsites, tethered animals and fires must be located at least 100 feet from lakes, streams and trails. In the Eagles Nest, no fires are allowed within 0.25 miles of lakes (stoves o.k.). No fires are allowed above timberline or in krummholz or riparian areas. Motorized vehicles and equipment of any kind, landing of aircraft or air drop of persons or supplies are prohibited. Erase all signs of campfires. Better yet, use a propane stove.

TIPS FOR HIKERS:
 Your Safety...
 Eagle County has a 911 emergency call system. Dispatch a fellow hiker to dial 911 for any emergency.

Altitude sickness first strikes with headache, listlessness, lack of appetite and nausea. At 10,000 feet, air contains only two-thirds the oxygen it has at sea level. Plus, the higher air pressure at sea level easily forces oxygen through the lung lining to the blood stream. Here, air pressure—and lung oxygen efficiency—are less. Avoid sudden trips to higher altitude. Take time to acclimate.

Avoid hiking alone, If you must, always leave trail route and anticipated return time with a family member or friend. If plans change, leave a clearly printed note in your car.

Hypothermia lowers body core temperature. Watch for shivering, slow slurred speech, fumbling hands, stumbling. Give hot drinks (no alcohol) and keep the victim warm and dry. Most hypothermia cases develop in 30 to 50 degree (not frigid) temperatures when the victim becomes wet. Put on rain gear before you get wet.

Even clear cold streams and lakes can harbor *Giardia lamblia,* a nasty organism that attacks the intestinal tract. To purify, boil water at least 15 minutes. Sophisticated chemical purifiers will kill *Giardia.* These germicides contain tetraglycine hydroperiodide and titratable iodine. *Giardia lamblia* is mainly caused by improper human waste disposal.

Electrical storms above timberline threaten hikers' lives. Lightning strikes and hazardous ground currents are deadly. When you see a thunderstorm brewing, turn back. Avoid electrical storms by starting the hike first thing in the morning. Storms usually begin in the early afternoon.

To warm up before a longer hike, use stretching exercises. Bob Anderson's *Stretching*, Shelter Publications, 1980 provides specific hiking warm-ups that can help to prevent problems such as painful inflamed knee cartilage.

 The Environment...
 At high elevations, food waste does not biodegrade. Eggshells, orange peels and other picnic refuse remains. Animals don't each such foods. Food, paper, foil and aluminum cans belong in the litter bag. Pack it in-Pack it out!

Outdoor lovers help protect flowers by refraining from picking them and animals by quietly keeping their distance. Hikers can protect fragile alpine tundra by walking on rocks or snow. Trail erosion is diminished when hikers stay on trails. Avoid short-cutting switchbacks, which forms a path for water erosion. Remind others to stay on the trail. Especially during damp periods, hikers can cause havoc to vulnerable forest and alpine terrain. Remember to camp well away from lakes and waterways. Fire rings are no longer acceptable, they mar the alpine environment. Bury all human waste. People one asked "Can man survive in the wilderness?" Today the question has become "Can the wilderness survive man?"

SKI TOURING/SNOWSHOEING:
Thirty trails or trail accesses in this book offer a delightful winter sports experience. The Vail area's powdery snow makes touring a physical pleasure, while mountain scenery provides a feast for the spirit. Driving directions for hikers will also bring skiers/snowshoers to winter trailheads. Snowshoers can use some of the hiking-only trails if they are careful of avalanche danger.

Remember that steep treeless slopes threaten avalanche danger. Crossing a dangerous slope invites trouble. If you must traverse near a steep open slope, especially one with a convex or rounded contour, travel either on the windward side of the ridge above the slope or well out in the valley below the slope. Avoid cornices and other "false ground" created by wind deposits of snow on leeward slopes. Call Colorado Avalanche Information Center (303) 275-5364 (Denver) for current data on mountain weather, snow and avalanche conditions 24 hours daily, November 15-May 1. The local 24-hour avalanche information number is 479-4652. Or visit the U.S. Forest Service office at Minturn or Eagle to obtain avalanche reports. In general, avoid skiing alone and traversing open slopes during or after a blizzard. Count windward slopes as more safe than leeward.

Clothing for back country users should be layered: "Breathable" long underwear *(ventilation)*, covered by a layer of wool shirt and pants *(insulation)*, then a wind and water-proof suit *(protection)* that covers head, neck and legs.

Winter touring at Eagle County's altitude requires plenty of liquids to offset fluid losses through rapid respiration in dry air. Fluids not only help to maintain energy levels but actually work to keep the body warmer. Alcohol and smoking shut down the capillaries, restricting blood flow to extremities.

CAMPGROUNDS:
Holy Cross Ranger District campgrounds include Gore Creek on the old Vail Pass highway; Camp Hale Memorial, Blodgett and Gold Park below Tennessee Pass; Hornsilver and Tigiwon south of Minturn. All open June 1 and close September 10, except Tigiwon at 9,900 feet elevation, which opens June 15. Camp Hale is biggest with 21 campsites; Blodgett smallest, has six. Fees are required at all but Tigiwon which has no services except toilet. All have fireplaces, tables, toilets and drinking water.

A FEW YEARS DOWN THE TRAIL:
The wild beauty of the Sawatch Range near Tennessee Pass, and the almost fairy-tale setting of its lake-dappled bowls, canyons and valleys, face devastation by the Aurora-Colorado Springs Homestake water diversion project. Homestake has already blemished this mountain Eden with roadways, huge metallic pipelines, concrete grids and soil disturbances. More diversion threatens to diminish streams and further ravage Eagle County's precious natural resources of mountain environment around the Homestake Reservoir.

HELP UPDATE THIS BOOK:
Though these 50 trails were researched recently, routes can change when rock slides, avalanches or other natural reversals occur, or when officials who

maintain trails construct alternate routes. Sometimes, hikers themselves will establish or change a trail. Help update, correct or add to this guide. Write to L. J. Gilliland, Publisher, Alpenrose Press, Box 499, Silverthorne, Colorado 80498.

DISTRICT RANGER STATIONS:

Holy Cross District
24747 U.S. Hwy 24(Box 190)
Minturn, CO 81645
(970)827-5715

Eagle District
125 W. 5th Street (Box 720)
Eagle, CO 81631
(970)328-6388

Check Our Web Site for These Backcountry Tips

Trail of the Week! Each week, author Mary Ellen Gilliland, selects the primo Vail-area trail for the week, summer or winter. Summer trails featured will offer the peak flowers, waterfall volume, wildlife viewing or berry-picking. Winter trails will offer top snow conditions, storm protection or insider getaways. Gilliland posts the weekly route on her wilderness-recreation web site at:

www.alpenrosepress.com

Just click on THE VAIL HIKER. You'll also find tips for neighboring Summit County by clicking on "The New Summit Hiker."

High Altitude Tips! You'll also find tips for avoiding altitude sickness, guarding against giardia and what to carry in your pack this week.

Cairns (rock piles used as trail markers) guide hikers, especially above timberline when snow hides the trail. These cairns on the grassy meadow atop Notch Mountain attempt to compete with Ten Mile Range beyond.

Trails in East Vail - Gore Range Wilderness

1   BOOTH FALLS AND LAKE

Falls:	Lake:
Time: 2-3 hours	**Time: 7 hours**
Distance: 2 miles	**Distance: 6 miles**
Elevation gain: 1,400 feet	**Elevation gain: 3,080 feet**
High point: 9,400 feet	**High point: 11,480 feet**
Rating: Moderate	**Rating: More difficult**
Usually open: June-October	**Usually open: July-mid-September**
Topo: USGS Vail East, 1987	

Yes, there is a heaven and it's tucked away up Booth Creek. Waterfalls (try to count 'em) include 60-foot Booth Falls at two miles where a crystal cataract gleams diamond-like against black rock. Beyond the falls, find Switzerland transported to the Rockies—flower-dotted subalpine meadows, green carpeted clefts, stunning views. The tarn, in a circle of moss rock and pink quartz, is a haven for hikers—and the curious marmot.

Drive 0.9 miles west from I-70 East Vail exit 180 to Booth Falls Road. Turn right and proceed to road's end to park. Arrive early—space is tight. Or, ride the bus to 0.2 miles below the trailhead.

The trail climbs north through aspen in a steep start, then levels to a gradual ascent through clover-scented woodland. In July, look for Colorado's state flower, the columbine, along with mariposa lily. After quite a stretch here, emerge into a long, crevice-shaped meadow with abundant wild-flowers—foothills paintbrush, yarrow, harebell, butter and eggs, larkspur, monks hood. Soon, trek a steep but quick slope to the Falls. Stay left amid the many side trails here. Booth Falls, a refreshing stop, is a popular destination.

Relocate the main trail and hike alongside the creek before climbing northeast into a deep conifer forest. The stream reappears, running alongside the trail. Look here for the elusive star-flowered pyrola (wood nymph), a white, waxy, close-to-the-ground blossom. As you move into the meadows, notice the trail fork (second meadow, just above 10,200 feet) where a footpath at left provides access to the Piney Lakes region via the Piney Creek Trail. Up higher, you can spot the green saddle where the advanced trail crosses over.

As the trees thin, the terrain changes constantly, providing views to the jumbled Gore Range ridges above, fields of flowers below, dozens of waterfalls and a trail that winds through green gorges and valleys. The final climb to the lake is relentless. Good boots pay off here. But flowers—rosy paintbrush, elephant head, queens crown, yellow monkey flower and Parry's primrose, plus fringed later-season gentian and star gentian—provide a feast for the eyes.

Booth Lake, at 11,480 feet, is big by alpine tarn standards and boasts an island plus good fishing. Rocks above offer a smooth spot for picnicking but watch the cold wind. Find protected campsites in the woods below.

Rolling rocks on the trail back to timberline demand caution on the trip down. As you approach the Vail valley, you may want to muse upon the area's history: Charlie Baldauf, a miner from silver and zinc-rich Gilman, built an early-day cabin at Booth Creek's mouth. Baldauf used hard-rock mining techniques to prepare his building site—he blasted out willow shrubs and boulders with dynamite. The Vail Mountain School has renovated Charlie's homestead and occupies it today.

Dazzling flower meadows and a multitude of little waterfalls enhance the trail that ends here at 11,480 foot Booth Lake.

The East Vail trails share common traits: Steepness, poor trail conditions, popularity, primitive grandeur and incredible beauty.

Praise the Lord from the heavens, praise him in the heights. Ps. 148:1

2   BOOTH CREEK BASIN^{TM}

Time: 5 hours
Distance: 5 miles
Elevation gain: 3,160 feet (basin)
High point: 11,400 (to basin); 11,760 (to pass)
Rating: Most difficult
Usually open: July–September
Topo: USGS Vail East

Looking for a wild alpine gorge? Eagle County mushroomed by 90 percent in the prosperous '90s, so a hikers retreat may be hard to find. But Booth Creek Basin^{TM}, an untamed drainage parallel to the Booth Lake bowl, lures advanced hikers with its solitude. Negatives include a shorts-ripping scramble over deadfall and a maddening trail. Positives include wild beauty in a lush pocket high in the Gore Range.

Drive to the trailhead using directions for Booth Lake, trail no. 1.

The trail follows the Booth Falls and Lake route for 3 miles, then turns 90 degrees left onto a blurred (at this writing) side trail. To find this side trail, hike about 1 mile past the waterfalls through deep conifer forest and then emerge into an open meadow. Drop down to cross the creek, and continue through the meadow about 0.2 miles. Before the trail disappears into another conifer forest, (about 85% across the rolling meadow), a faint trail appears at left. (We built a small cairn here, but it may be gone.) Take this trail, which the meadow grasses could conceal in a wet year, into the mouth of a side canyon.

Immediately huge fallen trees present a barrier to progress. Moreover, they disguise the trail. Look to see where the trail should go, and target that route as you clamber through the maze of downed timber. Rediscover the trail, only to encounter more windfall. Finally, the trail clears. Still, expect to lose the path now and then. Just remember that it stays right of the creek.

The footpath follows an embankment with the creek rushing below, then drops to continue alongside the roiling stream. Several idyllic picnic spots appear streamside.

Exit the trees to meet a big, green basin, lush with flowers in season. The trail cuts through subalpine meadows, then leads hikers northeast toward the headwall where it scales the ridge on its right side.

The valley's end serves as a destination. Or, you can attack the 11,760-foot pass for incomparable views of both the Crater Lake area (see trail no. 39) and the Piney River country (trails 37 and 38). The route over the headwall crosses to the Piney River drainage, past the Fly and the Spider, to Upper Piney Lake. From there, backpackers can link into the 9-mile trail down to Lower Piney Lake and Piney River Ranch along the Red Sandstone Road.

Booth Mountain, 12,163 feet, dominates this untamed basin. Advanced hikers can explore both the West Booth Pass gorge east of Booth Mountain and the Druid Pass bowl southwest of Booth Mountain.

The steep rock wall deserves some admiration: Like most of the Gore Range, it's made of 600-million-year-old Precambrian granite and gneiss. Despite crashing waves of an ancient inland sea, eons of rain and snow storms, plus bulldozer glaciers, it stands. Its rugged spine still snags the sky.

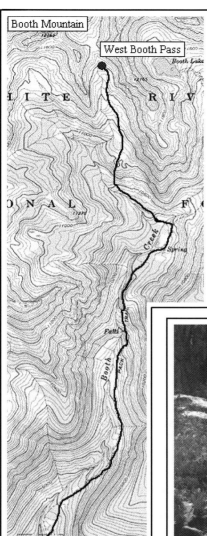

Booth Mountain

West Booth Pass

Stay right of the creek in Booth Creek Basin. Willows near streams provide both food and shelter for the tundra's only year-round bird resident, the ptarmigan. They live under the snow in winter, eating energy-rich willow twigs. Unlike other birds, the ptarmigan grow fat on their winter diet. Well camouflaged, the bird is pure white in winter and mottled brown in summer. Look for ptarmigan as you hike the upper basin.

Map printed from TOPO! National Geographic Holdings (*www.topo.com*)

3   PITKIN LAKE

Time: 7-8 hours
Distance: 5 miles
Elevation gain: 3,000 feet
High point: 11,400 feet
Rating: Most difficult
Usually open: July-September
Topo: USGS Vail East, 1987

A perverse trail into an alpine paradise--that's Pitkin. The trail is steep, slippery with dry silt and "ball bearing" rocks. You'll need boots with a great tread. But the scenery is stunning. Two beautiful waterfalls entice you along a winding trail that leads to Pitkin Lake, set in against a dramatic backdrop of raw glacier-carved granite. Rainbow-colored wildflowers and a myriad of butterflies delight the senses enroute.

Drive to East Vail I-70 exit 180 and go north under the highway to a road that heads uphill east. The short road, access to townhouses, parallels I-70. Park below the homes at right. The trailhead lies just past the creek crossing.

The trail begins with what some guidebooks would call "an exhilarating climb." It will warm you up. After about 10 minutes uphill, the trail forks. Go left. Watch for a 90-degree left turn next to some rocks that invite a rest stop. Now the trail gets steep. However, you do eventually emerge to a more moderate ascent through alternating aspen groves and flower meadows. Look for columbine, mariposa lily, harebell and chimingbell in July, gentian in August. When you enter the pine forest, you may see the dainty red "elegant" columbine which blooms in June. Beyond is a nice opening on Pitkin Creek for rest/snack breaks. There's talk of 10-12 inch brook and native trout here.

At 1.5 miles, cross the first of six small streams. Just past the final stream crossing at 10,000 feet altitude is the first of two waterfalls along the trail. Look for it about 200 feet east of the path—a great destination for a short hike.

Continuing hikers walk through a bog enroute to the second falls west of the trail at 10,460 feet. Cross Pitkin Creek and climb sharply. The trail then traverses stream-laced meadowlands, dotted with ponds.

Beautiful but frustrating, the terrain teases hikers from here on. Because the valley floor is convoluted and the trail twisted, the lake is always "beyond that rise." (It's not.) Our party took four hours to reach Pitkin Lake. Perfect for wading to cool sore feet, the lake pools beneath a dramatic cirque. Staggering 13,057 foot East Partner guards the bowl's east flank and 13,041 foot West Partner the north. (These peak names are unofficial names popularized by Colorado Mountain Club veteran mountaineer, Robert M. Ormes.)

This wild hanging valley bears the name of Colorado Governor Frederick W. Pitkin who served in the late 1870s. Perhaps the hob-nailed boots of his era would prove handy for negotiating the steep lower trail section on the return. Talcum-powder dust and roller-skate pebbles make slipping a hazard here. These annoyances pale however against the fact that Pitkin rivals Booth as most beautiful trail in the East Vail Eagles Nest Wilderness.

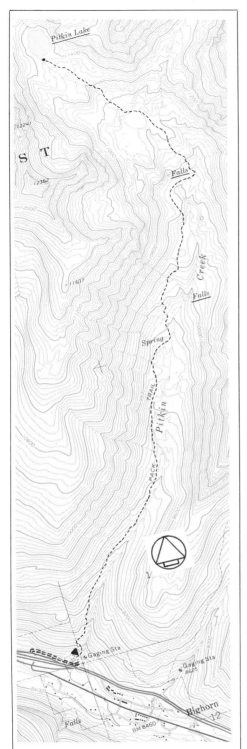

Variety of terrain--from aspen glades to wildflower gardens to convoluted mounds and benches of rock--characterizes the Pitkin trail.

4   BIGHORN CABIN

Time: 6 hours
Distance: 3.6 miles
Elevation gain: 2,200 feet
High point: 10,800 feet
Rating: More difficult
Usually open: Mid-June-September
Topo: USGS Vail East, 1987

Fluttering aspen, fern groves and flowers punctuate the trek to the "Bighorn Hilton," an early day homestead cabin. The homestead's back yard, just beyond the intact cabin, is a haven for wildflower fans. Brilliant splashes of pink paintbrush, Parry's primrose and rosy queens crown leap from a wet meadow of vivid green. Though private property, Olive Goodale's circa-1925 retreat remains unlocked as a storm shelter.

Drive on the south frontage road east 0.7 miles from I-70 East Vail interchange 180 to Columbine Drive. Turn left and proceed through a highway underpass 0.2 miles to the trailhead. Parking is very limited. You may wish to arrange with a friend for drop-off and pick-up or ride the bus to .04 miles below the trailhead.

The trail scales the hillside at a stiff rate for the first 0.5 miles. Then it follows a pleasant grade through thick aspen and pine into the primitive Gore Range Wilderness.

Where the trail levels off, watch for signs of an old wagon road used by miners and homesteaders. You will walk through red firecracker penstamen, purple monks hood and blond yarrow in July and enjoy the valley's butterfly population. Soon, wade through acres of Bracken's fern, rarely seen among these high aspen woods. A nice opening onto Bighorn Creek provides a rest stop. Just beyond is a cool campsite among huge, ancient pines. A moment later, pass remains of an early silver camp, with ruins of several structures. To date these old buildings, look for the presence of square nails. Since round nails became available mostly after the 1880s, early structures can be identified by their square-nail construction.

A shorter hike for families or hikers with limited time is possible by continuing to a point just past the fern grove. There, two aspen trees at left "point" to a side trail on the right. It leads to a nice picnic spot, a rocky outcropping with plunging views to Bighorn Creek. (Watch the kids.)

Continuing hikers will encounter the first of two rock fields. In the first, continue straight ahead, then veer right to pick up the trail. Watch for cairns (rocks piled as markers). In the second rock field, stay right.

Get ready for great views at mile 2. Sweeping vistas down the valley to Vail compete for attention with the white cascade of Bighorn Falls on the cliff wall at left. Note thick pockets of Colorado's state flower, the blue columbine, in late June and early July.

Now trek over a lung-buster ridge that divides the lower and upper valleys. Rewards are Indian paintbrush, red as a circus lady's lipstick, and a level wooded trail to the cabin beyond. Idyllic in its setting, the cabin is dwarfed by surrounding peaks.

Aggressive hikers can access the Grand Traverse from upper Bighorn. This dizzying route, a continuous ridge at 12,000 feet, connects this area's Gore Range peaks and high drainages. Stay on the creek's right fork and head northeast for 12,340-foot Central Pass which provides access to Summit

County's Rock Creek drainage. (For Rock Creek see Mary Ellen Gilliland's guide, *The New Summit Hiker*, Alpenrose Press, 1995.) Just below the cabin lies an unmarked route east over the East Traverse to Deluge Creek. These routes are extremely steep and hazardous, for experts only.

September along beautiful Bighorn Creek offers a golden retreat to quiet. Less steep than other East Vail hikes, the Bighorn trail is generally smooth and easy to walk.

Hikers can enjoy nice views back to East Vail from rocky outcropping just past the fern grove, a good picnic spot.

5   DELUGE LAKE

Time: 7-8 hours
Distance: 4 miles
Elevation gain: 3,085 feet
High point: 11,765 feet
Rating: Most difficult
Usually open: July-September
Topo: USGS Vail East, 1987

Wild. Remote. Untouched. The inner reaches of the steep Deluge Creek drainage offer isolation and primitive grandeur. Eden-like flower meadows yield to a placid lake resting beneath Gore Range granite. Hikers earn all these rewards on a wilderness trail both beautiful and demanding.

Drive east from East Vail I-70 exit 180 on the south frontage road 2.3 miles to the Gore Creek trailhead on the road's left side. Gore Creek Campground is just beyond. Park at the trailhead or on the road above.

The trail begins on the Gore Creek footpath. Almost immediately (0.1 miles) turn left at the fork for the narrow Deluge trail which heads north through waist-high vegetation. Soon the path curves to follow the northeast direction it will take all the way to Deluge Lake at 4 miles. The Gore Creek Trail (see hikes 6, 7 and 8) goes east to a junction with the Gore Lake route and continues to 11,740-foot Red Buffalo Pass.

The trail intersects with two game trails going downhill east. The Deluge trail climbs northeast, passes through several boulder fields, and then clings to a very steep slope as it climbs through aspen woods. Use extreme caution here. Don't step off the trail's downhill side to let other hikers pass. Vegetation hides the hill's true grade.

A challenging climb, punctuated by the refreshing chill of dark pine forest, puts you high enough to enjoy an eagle's view of East Vail behind. Above stretches a panorama of jagged Gore Range peaks and ridges. The pass visible is an unnamed crossing dubbed "Snow Lake Pass" by hikers. Below lies the startling plunge to Deluge Creek.

Flowers abound along this trail. At lower elevations look for mariposa lily, cow parsnip, harebell, wild geranium, umbrella buckwheat, rosy pussytoes. In the pines, note Jacob's ladder, a pretty short-stemmed purple cluster with ladder-like leaves. On the July tundra near Deluge Lake, discover "belly flowers," the ground-clinging miniature blooms you see best from a prone position. Alpine flowers found here include white alpine sandwort, pink moss campion and the blue-blue alpine forget-me-not. Wildlife—elk, deer and ptarmigan—also flourish here.

The trail drops to Deluge Creek at 3.25 miles and a wet garden of pink Parry's primrose, yellow monkeyflower, white brook cress. Walk alongside the creek's left side and watch for cairns to point out the tricky spot where the boggy trail crosses to Deluge Creek's right (east) side.

Cross the creek and note this spot for reference on the return. Walk a gentle grade now as the trail ascends toward timberline. A cabin, on private land, offers shelter to hikers. Cairns mark the trail as it approaches Deluge Lake. Views to the Sawatch and Mount of the Holy Cross emerge. Rolling contours hide the tarn. If in doubt, follow the creek up.

On the return: 0.75 miles below, near where the trail crosses Deluge Creek, avoid a route straight ahead where confused hikers have beaten a path. Look for two cairns, one on each side of the stream. Soon after the crossing, note a fork. One branch goes downhill left. The Deluge trail goes uphill right.

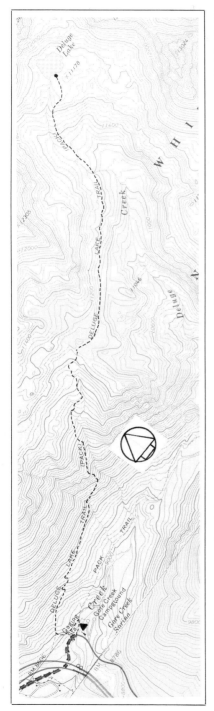

A green alpine garden stretches like carpet to water's edge at Deluge Lake. A snowfield feeding the lake insures the water's icy nip.

Isolated and unspoiled, Deluge Lake nestles beneath an arc of raw granite. Southern sun bathes the trail so autumn hiking is pleasant.

Time: 10 hours
Distance: 15.7 miles
Elevation gain: 2,520 feet
High point: 11,740 feet
Rating: Most difficult
Usually open: July-mid-September
Topo: Trails Illustrated - Vail, Frisco, Dillon

A natural link between Vail and its neighbor, Summit County, Red Buffalo Pass provides splendid views on a demanding all-day outing. Once considered instead of Vail Pass as the I-70 route, the crossing is best hiked from the east due to a steep western wall. Heavily tramped by miners' boots a century earlier, this historic byway, formerly called Wilkinson Pass, remains remote, untrodden and beautiful today.

Two cars are required. Leave one car at the Gore Creek Campground, 2.3 miles east of I-70 East Vail exit 180 on the south frontage road.

Drive a second car to the trailhead above Silverthorne. Take Colorado 9 north from I-70 Silverthorne exit 205 to the Wildernest Road at the 7-11 store corner across from Wendy's. The trailhead is in Mesa Cortina, 1.6 miles. Turn left and proceed to the fork. Turn right, then immediately left onto Royal Buffalo Drive (no. 1240). Drive 1 mile to Lakeview Drive (no. 1245); turn right. Proceed to a fork with Aspen Drive. Go left on Aspen, up and around a short distance to trailhead parking. A trail sign reads Mesa Cortina.

The trail rises gradually through meadow-pocketed aspen forest, then pine, to meet at 2.1 miles an old ranch road. Columbine, lupine, wild rose, harebell and the more rare mariposa lily grow here, as well as the red elegant columbine and unusual varieties of the violet. Native orchids sometimes blossom in the Wildernest-Mesa Cortina area as well. August brings many kinds of mushrooms, while September unleashes a splash of gold.

At 2.6 miles, meet South Willow Creek and the Gore Range Trail junction. The trail's left branch, your choice, mounts Red Buffalo Pass.

At 3.5 miles, hikers pass the intersection with the South Willow Trail and beyond that, at 4.2 miles, a short trail leading to commanding South Willow Creek Falls, a great rest stop at 10,200 feet. Note massive rock formations here. Soon after snowmelt you may find yellow glacier lilies below the pass.

Steep jagged slopes of Buffalo Mountain, left, and Red Peak, right, form a deep crevice as the trail continues. Later, the path curves south to intersect at 6.2 miles with the Gore Creek Trail from East Vail. It is your route. (The Gore Range Trail crosses the alpine bowl, dotted with shining ponds, to scale Eccles Pass to the south.) This hike will go right (northwest), meet the Gore Creek Trail, climb Red Buffalo Pass and cross to the Gore Range west slope.

Red Buffalo Pass, 11,740 feet, provides a falcon's view of the Gore Range and a long sweep into the broad Gore Creek valley leading to Vail.

The Gore Creek trail switchbacks from the grassy slope at the crest down to cross Gore Creek, passing a ruined cabin, a rock cairn and grassy meadow enroute. Shorter switchbacks follow the creek crossing, then the trail emerges from the woods to enter a large meadow at the edge of a basin. Stay left (southwest) and look for trail signs. Drop at a moderate grade through the woods. A large open area and two smaller clearings follow, then hikers balance on a log to cross rushing Gore Creek.

A sign indicates Gore-Willow Creek Pass before you veer left and walk to the Gore Lake Trail junction. Look for a grave, less than 50 yards from the creek crossing; it commemorates 1870s pioneers, the Recen brothers. (See p. 33.)

Another mile brings you to a large treeless section along the valley wall. Soon drop through woods and pass small, stagnant ponds. Cross Deluge Creek. The trail descends from evergreen forest to grass and aspen woods, then crosses a few shallow streams. A fine finish comes with the walk along Gore Creek, which thrusts itself headlong toward the valley floor, rushing over black boulders and and leaping over rock ledges. Finally, the trail drops down to the Gore Creek Campground, a long but rewarding walk and one you may not soon forget.

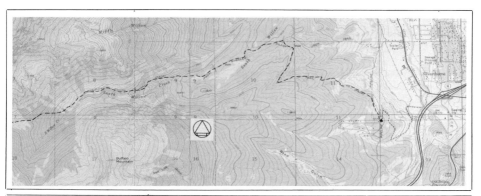

A butterfly lights on a flower on the 15.7-mile Red Buffalo Pass trail. The Summit County portion intrigues flower lovers with rarities such as wild orchids and history lovers with a ruined silver camp. The Vail side offers knee-deep flowers, butterflies and boisterous Gore Creek.

7   GORE CREEK

Time: 6 hours
Distance: 5 miles
Elevation gain: 1,440 feet
High point: 10,200 feet
Rating: Moderate
Usually open: Mid-June-September
Topo: Trails Illustrated - Vail, Frisco, Dillon

America's streets were paved with silver for two young Swedes, Daniel and Andrew Recen, who emigrated to Colorado in 1876. Dan promptly discovered the dazzling Queen of the West mine on Jacque Peak near Vail Pass. Andrew struck silver at the adjoining Enterprise Lode. Soon the brothers tarried with 1880s silver magnates such as H. A. W. Tabor and celebrities such as songbird Jenny Lind. The Recens hired private rail cars for bachelor parties and consumed champagne and oysters with extravagant regularity.

The Gore Creek hike takes you to the graves of this pair. After the 1893 silver crash, the Recens found themselves almost penniless. They hunted and trapped all through the Gores till their deaths in 1912 and 1917. Their graves lie near their longtime cabin site on Gore Creek.

Drive east 2.3 miles from East Vail I-70 exit 180 on the frontage road to the signed Gore Creek trailhead on the road's east side. Parking is available here as well as just above near the Gore Creek Campground. Gore Creek, a popular Eagles Nest Wilderness hike, may be heavily used on summer holidays and weekends. Go midweek.

The trail follows Gore Creek's north side along grassy slopes and aspen groves. Enjoy short climbs alongside whitewater cascades and walks along flower-strewn meadows where the creek meanders. The first section climbs the sun-bathed valley wall, with periodic short but steep ascents. Then the trail drops gently to cross several small streams. After a fairly level walk, the path parallels Gore Creek, then begins an irregular climb. Enter the conifer forest and cross Deluge Creek in a shady glen at near 2 miles.

Continue through forest, break onto an open slope, then climb through lodgepole pine. (Lodgepole, perhaps least lovely of the evergreens, is so named because of its use: Mountain-dwelling Utes, along with their plains neighbors, the Arapahoe and Cheyenne, prized the young straight pines for their use as teepee poles. Hence, "lodge" pole.)

Pass some dead ponds, then later traverse a treeless slope. After more woods at 4 miles you continue the last mile to stop at the junction with the Gore Lake Trail (a short but very steep 1.5 mile climb). Here, where your trail confronts a Gore Creek crossing, is your destination. (The footpath continues to Red Buffalo Pass, trail no. 6, a 15.7 mile route to Summit County best hiked from the other side.) The area provides plenty of good picnic sites and Gore Creek abounds in wily trout.

The Recen graves are just uphill at left. The brothers, who lived and died here, left a legacy in Colorado. When Dan died, his nephew from Frisco transported the body up here for burial. A fierce October blizzard struck enroute and the nephew, after digging the grave, waded through drifts all the way back to Frisco. Half-frozen and exhausted on arrival, he was cared for at Frisco's Excelsior mine till the weather permitted his return home.

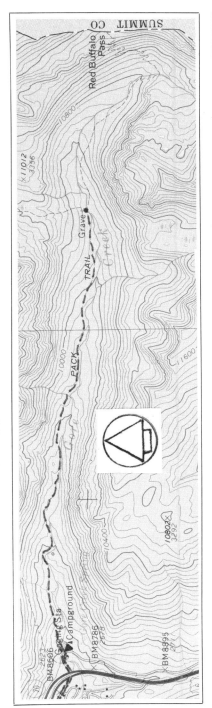

For a rewarding experience along popular Gore Creek hike mid-week and avoid hectic holiday weekends. This big, beautiful valley in the Gore Range/Eagles Nest Wilderness receives high use.

The Recen brothers, shown above, led lives that reflect the boom and bust cycle of Eagle County's mining era. A big flush followed Daniel's silver strikes at the Ten Mile Canyon town of Kokomo. Then the 1893 silver crash brought ruin. Local gold towns like Gold Park and Holy Cross City peaked and crashed.

8   GORE LAKE

Time: 9 hours
Distance: 6.5 miles
Elevation gain: 2,720 feet
High point: 11,400 feet
Rating: More difficult
Usually open: July-September
Topo: Trails Illustrated - Vail, Frisco, Dillon

Gore Lake, a tarn at timberline, is named for Sir St. George Gore, a rampaging Irish baronet who toured the Colorado Rockies in 1859 on a hunting safari. The well-heeled huntsman made such an impact here that the Gore Range, Gore Pass, Gore Lake, Summit County's 54.5 mile Gore Range Trail plus a bevy of lodges and restaurants bear his name. What Lord Gore termed "sport" we would label slaughter, for the nobleman massacred 2,000 buffalo, 1,600 elk and deer, 100 bear along with countless antelope, small game and fish. Lord Gore never visited this alpine lake—perhaps it's just as well!

Drive 2.3 miles from East Vail I-70 exit 180 east on the south frontage road to the marked Gore Creek trailhead. Park here, or on crowded summer weekends and holidays, park above the Gore Creek Campground just beyond.

The trail maintains a pleasant grade throughout its first five-mile section on the Gore Creek Trail. After the intersection with the Gore Lake Trail, however, the trail scales 1,160 feet in just 1.5 miles—a stiff climb. Just 0.25 miles from the trailhead enter the Gore Range Wilderness, a 133,496-acre federally protected primitive area.

Follow the trail directions for the Gore Creek Trail to the Recen brothers' gravesite at mile 5. Here, at the junction with the Gore Lake Trail, take a sharp left up the hill. The route winds upward next to a roaring stream, a sharp climb for the first 0.5 miles. After 0.75 miles cross a small watercourse and catch your breath among the several wildflower-dotted meadows here. These lush basins are worth a pause. The uphill trek intensifies as you reach scattered trees and finally a bench just east of the lake. One of the prettiest of the east Vail lakes, Gore sparkles amid a setting of spruce and fir, with jagged Gore peaks above.

After a cold spring, Gore Lake can remain frozen till late June and broken snowfields can hamper progress. If these conditions exist, be sure to bring a topo map along because the lake can be tricky to find when the trail is hidden. Look for the elusive glacier lily when snow lingers. This yellow blossom, often finished blooming before hiking season begins, flourishes near Gore Lake.

Campers planning to overnight at Gore Lake probably will do so without the flair demonstrated by Lord Gore. He traveled the rugged Rockies with unparalleled camp luxury. His gay green and white striped tent housed an oval bathtub, handwoven French carpet, British campaign chests and fine leather trunks, indoor camp stove, folding table and chairs, library of leather-bound first-edition books and antique gun racks. Another portable luxury: A solid brass bed. And no "room with a path" for the baronet. Instead, two wigged and liveried British valets placed at the foot of Lord Gore's brass bed an elegant fur-lined commode.

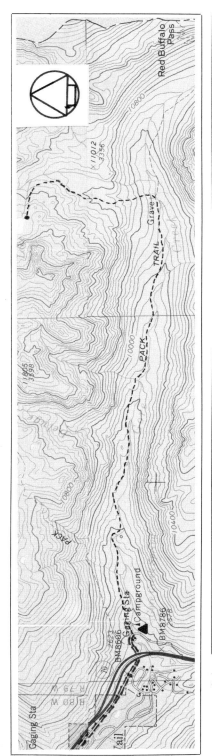

Gore Lake, an alpine tarn just below timberline, bears the name of lordly huntsman, Sir St. George Gore. His grand safari guided by famous hunter-trapper Jim Bridger came as close as nearby Grand County. The baronet read Shakespeare to Bridger who labeled the Oxford-educated lord as "too high-falutin' for me."

Parry's primrose, grows on mossy "islands" on Gore Creek's tributaries.

Trails on Vail Pass

9   OLD VAIL PASS

To Polk Creek:
Time: 3-4 hours
Distance: 3.5 miles
Elevation gain: 940 feet
High point: 9,680 feet
Rating: Easy
Usually open: May-September
Topo: Trails Illustrated - Vail, Frisco, Dillon

Kids' Hike to Sandbar:
Time: Depends on kids
Distance: 0.5 miles
Elevation gain: 340 feet
High point: 8,800 feet
Rating: Easy
Usually open: July-September

An easy hike for families with young children, seniors or visitors getting used to the altitude, the Old Vail Pass road provides plenty of fun. You can nibble wild raspberries in August, take kids to a shallow sand bar on Black Gore Creek or tote a picnic to peaceful Polk Creek.

Drive 2.3 miles from East Vail I-70 exit 180 east on the south frontage road to the highway closure. Park and go through the motor vehicle closure gate.

The trail is Charles D. Vail's 1940-engineered Vail Pass road which served as Vail's sole east-west highway access until I-70 completion. In August, 1980 the state dedicated this route as the Vail Pass-Ten Mile Canyon Recreation Trail for multi-purpose use including "family activities, running and bicycling." Although hikers share the road with bikers, it is wide enough for both. The trail winds gently upward to end just above Polk Creek, where the road quits and a two-lane bikeway continues over Vail Pass on a 30-mile route to Frisco.

Kids' Hike: Families walking to the sandy Black Gore Creek play area will follow the roadway 0.5 miles to beyond the I-70 highway sign that reads "Truck Ramp 2000 feet." On the creek below right is a shallow-water sand bar, great for kids with sand pails and shovels. (Note: This area is dangerous for children during spring run-off or during periodic high water times, including rainy seasons or sudden heavy showers.)

Find raspberries on the highway side of the path here and the plentiful purple-blue harebell. A showy July blossom is the three-foot high common mullein with fuzzy pale green leaves and clustered yellow petals. Two miles from the gate continuing hikers will see the Two Elk trailhead (no. 10). Try a walk down to the wooden bridge over Black Gore Creek, a cool, shady oasis.

The road, which begins above the lower I-70 truck runaway ramp ends at the upper runaway ramp. Just before you reach the dead end, you will see the deep Polk Creek canyon on your left. The creek's west hillside makes a great lunch spot. You can watch for beavers, active here, and enjoy views of the sheer-drop red sandstone cliff above rushing, evergreen-lined Polk Creek.

Charles D. Vail, the route's namesake, earned the labels of "tempestuous" and "headstrong" during his stint as Colorado Highway Department director. He "bulldozed his way through government officials" with the same ease he bulldozed many Colorado mountain passes. When this balding, bespectacled bulldog named a Salida-area pass after himself, Salida residents got mad. They went so far as to paint out the "P" on the Vail Pass signs he erected. Finally, that embattled pass was renamed Monarch Pass. Highway officials found a little-known crossing to bear the public servant's name—today's Vail Pass.

Ski Touring/Snowshoeing (Easy): Drive 1.9 miles from I-70 exit 180 to the end of the plowed frontage road just past Main Gore Drive. Ski or snowshoe 0.4 miles toward the bike path gate. (Snow may be thin under the highway bridge.) Pass the Gore Creek trailhead and campground but don't tour that drainage due to avalanche danger. The old Vail Pass route makes a delightful mid-winter jaunt, gradual and scenic. A moonlight tour on the evening of the full moon during December, January or February provides great views of starry skies and the jeweled lights of East Vail below. Take this tour during the true winter months; early winter snows are thin and March sun may burn off the snow-covered pavement. (Every rule has its exception: In some years, this trail keeps good snow through April.)

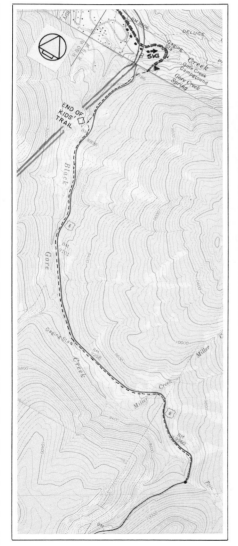

Gentle in its beauty, the rolling Old Vail Pass Road follows a historic route used by nomad Ute Indians. Once called "Pottery Pass" for its Indian pottery fragments, the road leads to an Indian hunting ground where radio-carbon-dated arrowheads and hunting implements date back to 4,800 B.C.

The heavens declare the glory of God; the skies proclaim the work of his hands. Ps. 19:11

37

10   TWO ELK

Time: 6-8 hours
Distance: 11 miles
Elevation gain: 2,300 feet
High point: 11,000 feet
Rating: Moderate
Usually open: July-September
Topo: USGS Vail East, 1987

Kids' Hike (to third bridge):
Time: 3 hours
Distance: 2.8 miles
Elevation gain: 700 feet
High point: 9,400 feet
Rating: Easy
Usually open: July-Sept.

Two Elk is a National Recreation Trail, a status reserved for especially scenic, historic and varied routes. Two Elk meets the criteria with its staggering Gore Range views, its Holy Cross vista and its constantly changing terrain. From the start in a closed-in canyon on a sparkling creek to its meadowed top-of-the-world summit and descent through a lush valley, Two Elk ranks as one of the Vail area's special hikes. Choose a clear day to enjoy the views.

Two cars are required for the longer hike. (Just one for the Kids' Hike.) Leave one car south of Minturn: Drive U.S. 24 2.7 miles past I-70 exit 171 to the bridge spanning the Eagle River. Turn left, cross the bridge and tracks, then proceed south past the cemetery. Go right at the first fork and left at the second fork. This Denver and Rio Grande access road is a somewhat rough dirt road. Follow it about 1.8 miles and park near the obvious mouth of Two Elk Canyon. The trail will come out beside Two Elk Creek at a point below the clearly-seen gas pipeline cut on the steep slope to the south.

Drive the second car (or the car for the Kids' Hike) 2.3 miles east from I-70 East Vail exit 180 on the south frontage road. Pass the Gore Creek Campground and park just beyond at the road closure gate. Walk 1.8 miles up the old Vail Pass road, today's recreational path, to the Two Elk trailhead at right.

The trail drops to a bridge crossing of boisterous Black Gore Creek, then passes under I-70 into the tight Timber Creek canyon. Watch for a deep hole in the trail just where you step onto the bridge and for a trail fork where you go left. The next delightful section of the trail keeps you in cool shady forest alongside the smooth-flowing creek. Note the red-rock slabs in the creek bottom, quite different from the rocky creekbeds often seen.

The Kids' Hike ends at 2.8 miles where the trail turns a sharp right across a third bridge to climb a steep hillside. Use the bridge area for rest and play.

At this third bridge the continuing trail swings southwest to mount a grassy slope, then scales a steep pine-forested hill. Much of the altitude gain (roughly 1,600 feet) happens on this 1.8 mile climb. A knockout view awaits you at the summit. A panorama of the Gore Range's East Vail peaks stretches in grandeur. To the northwest lie the softer contours of Vail Mountain's famous back bowls, Mongolia, Siberia, China, Sunup, Sundown and Game Creek; southwest is Blue Sky Basin. Southeast are peaks of the Sawatch Range. An Indian name, "Sawatch" (Saguache) means "water of the blue earth."

From the open, grassy Two Elk Pass summit, drop down to wide meadows with sweeping Sawatch views. Look for the Mount of the Holy Cross here. Hikers may encounter flocks of sheep in these high meadows. A more sure bet is an encounter with mountain bikers.

As you approach the first trees, note the gray rock formations. Rocks offer intriguing variety on this trail. Hikers may be distracted by the trail's array of wildflowers and its sweeping views. But please don't miss the rocks. In the open meadows, trailside rock formations create pictures; one is clearly an eagle. Black mud-like rocks looking like volcanic ooze, appear as the trail cuts in close to the creek. Limestone, formed from the shells of ancient marine organisms, stands in 200-foot citadels on the cliffs near Minturn.

Vail's Blue Sky Basin expansion has altered the wilderness character of Two Elk valley. And the trail itself has been rerouted by development. But it's still worthwhile and downhill skiers will enjoy scoping out the Basin terrain.

Yellow monkey flower still blossoms in little streams up high and raspberries proliferate alongside the August trail lower down. The path undulates above and level with the creek, then enters the coolness of the aspen-pine. Cross a third bridge and then you're at trail's end, a sunny bench of cottonwood and aspen where the showy five-foot mullein blooms.

Ski Touring/Snowshoeing (Easy): The Old Vail Pass Road makes a delightful winter trek. (See directions for trail no. 9.) Another option is the Minturn access to Two Elk Canyon. You can drive (see directions above) to the U.S. Forest Service sign past the cemetery where the road forks, park and snowshoe or ski into the mouth of the Two Elk drainage, about 1.5 miles. Follow gas pipeline markers. Two Elk closes from May 1-July 1 for elk calving.

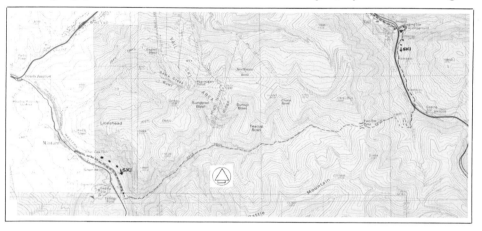

Begin the Two Elk Trail on Vail Pass to save an additional 1,000-foot climb necessary when the hike starts at Minturn. Prepare for neck-swiveling views. Drainages visible east below Eagles Nest Primitive Area peaks are Gore, Bighorn, Pitkin and Booth. To the west rise the Sawatch Range's massive mountains, including Mount Jackson and Mount of the Holy Cross. Bring a camera for both panoramic and close-up shots.

11   CORRAL CREEK

Time: 5 hours
Distance: 4 miles
Elevation gain: 1,640 feet
High point: 12,000 feet
Rating: Moderate
Usually open: Mid-July-September
Topo: USGS Vail Pass, 1987

The Corral Creek drainage hides a haven removed from the world. The green, stream-cut alpine bowl at the creek's head provides a garden-like retreat. The ridge above the bowl crests in Uneva Peak. It offers sweeping views to the mountains around Uneva Pass. Hikers gain all this with relative ease: The 4-mile hike covers mostly gradual terrain.

Drive to the I-70 Vail Pass summit, exit 190. Park at the rest area. Vail Pass, used as a Ute hunting camp for 6,000 years, offered archaeologists a trove of arrowheads, knives and scrapers during I-70 Vail Pass construction.

The trail begins on the bike path. Heading east, toward Copper Mountain, walk down the recreation path (cautiously, against bicycle traffic) for 1 mile. A wooden bridge spans Corral Creek here and a sign identifies the creek. You will cross under the massive I-70 highway bridge at left. Stay left as you pass beneath the bridge and veer left as you climb the hill to the meadow. Look for an old logging road that begins near the trees on the valley's west side. This road is the trail which heads north into Corral Creek.

Pass an old corral which gave the drainage its name and the modern communications structure. Deer abound in this valley; you may see several before hunting season begins. This logging road makes a fairly clear trail. If in doubt, keep the Copper Mountain ski runs behind you in this part of the walk. After an easy one-hour climb, a trail fork enters an "avenue" of evergreens at right. Avoid that and continue on the route till close to timberline.

Huge original-forest stumps in this area offer evidence of loggers' nirvana. When you emerge from the trees at timberline, look back to check your location so you can easily find the trail on the return trip.

Follow the edge of a rock flow around as you climb into a big alpine valley, still working toward the left or the northerly direction. Soon you can follow the creek up through a green wildflower-studded paradise. The creek begins as a spring. Above that is a footpath which heads uphill sharply northeast. Take the steep, short climb up Uneva Peak for a memorable view of Uneva Pass (see *The New Summit Hiker* by Mary Ellen Gilliland) and north to Chief Mountain. You can hike to Uneva Pass and Copper Mountain via the ridgeline, crossing Uneva Pass to access the Gore Range Trail heading south. Scan the Sawatch Range for the Holy Cross view.

The Ten Mile Range rises east. Behind lies the sweep of the Corral Creek valley and the Black Lakes pool below Vail Pass.

On your return, be aware that a recent new fork to the right will draw you downhill into a deep forest. This is a spur trail leading to the I-70 Vail Pass interchange. You can walk it as a shortcut to the rest area parking lot if you choose. Use caution on the highway if you go this way.

Ski Touring/Snowshoeing (More Difficult): Drive 0.7 miles west of the Vail Pass I-70 summit to the truck parking area. The tour begins here at 10,549 feet and provides a warming climb to almost 11,000 feet, then a pleasant downhill across wide, open slopes. The I-70 highway runs due north to Vail at this location. Bearing this in mid, climb east up to a long, rolling open area. Then turn north and ski or snowshoe this open corridor to a hill at 10,922 feet which is the high point before the slope drops off toward Vail. The thick conifer forest will be on the right almost all along. Uneva Peak will also be on the right just behind you at the high point. Do not venture east through the trees to the avalanche-prone slopes facing I-70. Skiers can enjoy a long sweet ride all the way to the hiking trailhead below Vail Pass at the confluence of Corral and West Tenmile Creeks, then climb 1.7 miles back to the truck stop. Or, enjoy a fast return glide directly to the parking area. Snowshoers will love the meadow-pocked stands of huge evergreens and often flawless snow. If the weather is stormy, find the protected logging road in the trees for your tour.

A high mountain bowl furnishes wild-flowers galore amid streams colored by brilliant moss colonies. Above look for krummholz, the shrubby, wind scarred "trees" that survive above timberline

Time: 6-7 hours
Distance: 7.6 miles
Elevation gain: 1,237 feet
High point: 11,700 feet
Rating: Moderate
Usually open: July-September
Topo: USGS Red Cliff, 1987

Treat yourself to spectacular Gore and Sawatch Range views on Bow-man's Shortcut, a trek that's well over 7 miles but mostly downhill. The trail follows a rolling grade to Two Elk Pass. Then it drops through forest to beautiful Timber Creek and emerges onto the Vail Pass recreation trail ending near Gore Creek Campground. Bring a map and compass for this hike. In winter, this trail begins the Commando Run, Colorado's top-rated ski tour, a challenging all-day excursion for experts only. (See page 120.) Be it July or January, you'll find it worthwhile to tote a camera.

Two cars are required: Leave one car at trail's end above the Gore Creek Campground. Drive 2.3 miles east from I-70 East Vail exit 180 on the south frontage road to the closure gate at the Vail Pass bikeway.

Drive a second car to the Vail Pass summit rest area and pick up the Shrine Pass Road, no. 709, just west of the exit. Shrine Pass, 11,050 feet, was the shortest (and toughest) route from Denver to Glenwood Springs before the Vail Pass road was built in 1940. Follow the Shrine Pass Road past a Holy Cross view sign at 3.75 miles. Continue to the junction with the Timber Creek Road at near 4.0 miles. Go right for 0.5 miles to an intersection with the Lime Creek Road, no. 728. Go left here 0.1 miles to the trailhead at right which is marked with a wooden pole inscribed "Colorado Trail." (The Colorado Trail has since taken a different route, using Kokomo Pass from Summit to Eagle County. See hikes 34 and 35.)

The trail begins on a level path through the woods, followed by a marked ascent. Views open up quickly: The glacier-carved Gore Range, visible from trail right, is displayed in all its jagged splendor. Copper Mountain's ski runs appear, with the massive Ten Mile Range as a backdrop.

Avoid a spur downhill right at less than 1 mile.

Emerge from woods to enter a large open meadow. The trail played out here in past years but a tread has reappeared with increased use. You may have to use map and compass in the meadow to follow the route. The trail goes north-northwest; use your compass and map to strike in that direction. Keep the Gore Range in view. (The tendency is to go downhill left, leaving the Gore view and the ridge. Wrong!)

Come to a wooden marker at meadow's end and pick up the trail again. Follow the ridge. Soon you'll encounter a major trail sign.

Passing this sign, proceed downhill right to pick up the trail. Drop into the trees, climb, then drop sharply to Two Elk Pass with its great photo opportunities. A sign points out the Two Elk Trail to Minturn (no. 10) and the 1.8 mile route to I-70 via Timber Creek. This hike follows the trail to I-70, which heads downhill east. After a steep downhill trek with occasional views to the Gore, traverse a hillside meadow to the creek.

A cool pleasant creek side walk brings you out of the narrow canyon, to pass under I-70 and climb a short hill to the paved old Vail Pass road, now a recreation trail. Turn left and walk 1.8 miles to the closure gate and your car.

Ski Touring (Most difficult): This 8-10 hour, 18-mile run challenges expert mountaineers to cope with map and compass, route selection, avalanche identification—and weather prediction (a clear day is required). Although increased use has made trail-finding easier by providing most groups a track or signs of a track, winds and storms can blot out trail evidence. Skiers may want to use the non-road skier-designated cross-country route for the Vail Pass area but take care to cross the indistinct summit and end up on the Shrine Pass Road near the Shrine Mountain Inn.

The trail divides itself into three sections. First the Shrine Pass-Lime Creek roads; second, Bowman's Shortcut to Two Elk Pass, and beyond to Pt. 11,816 (Red or "Siberia" Peak); third, the sweeping descent to the Vail Ski Mountain's Golden Peak runs.

For full directions and map, please turn to the appendix on page 120.

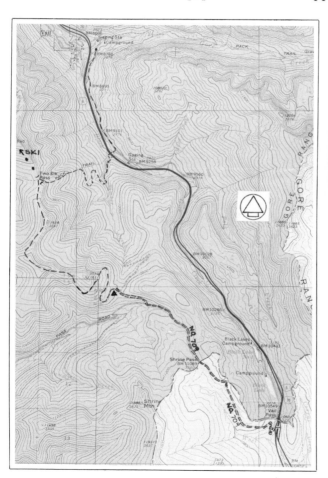

Hikers dance their way down easy "Bowman's," a moderate hike to lofty places. Skiers use the route for the demanding Commando Run, but don't descend the avalanche-prone slope to Vail Pass. Instead, ski touring groups continue north then northwest past powder-blessed Mushroom bowl to Vail.

13   COMMANDO RIDGE™

Time: 5-7 hours
Distance: 10 miles
Elevation gain: 1,700 feet
High point: 11,800 feet
Rating: More difficult
Usually open: July-September
Topo: USGS Red Cliff

A ridge that slices the sky at above 11,000 feet provides a memory-maker walk from the Vail Pass area to the Vail ski mountain base. Staggering views of the sawtooth Gore range, the soaring Sawatch Range and Vail's storied back bowls leave hikers satiated by panoramas. An all-day outing, the Commando Ridge™ trail requires a clear day to take full advantage of its huge views. Warning: don't bump your head on the stratosphere.

Two cars are necessary. Leave one at Vail's Golden Peak parking lot on the east side of the village on Vail Valley Road.

Drive using directions for Bowman's Shortcut, trail no. 12.

The trail enters the Englemann spruce forest on a level footpath before beginning a rousing climb. Avoid a fork downhill right at less than 1.0 mile. Along the 900-foot ascent to Two Elk Pass, forest windows open to the icepick Gore Range at right. The ski runs you notice belong to Summit County's Copper Mountain, a backdrop to the ancient Ten Mile Range.

Later, the route leads north-northwest (and the direction seems wrong) through a big alpine meadow, then penetrates deep woods as it eventually drops to Two Elk Pass. This open saddle at 11,000 feet delivers big views west across Vail's back bowls and Blue Sky Basin to the Sawatch Range summits.

Several trails intersect at Two Elk Pass. The Bowman's Shortcut trail makes a steep plunge north (right) to I-70, the bikeway and the Gore Creek Campground. The Two Elk Trail, a National Scenic Trail, descends west (left) into the beautiful creek valley below. The Commando Run—a famed winter ski trail used by World War II skiing soldiers and the partial route of this hike, Commando Ridge™continues straight ahead.

Your goal is the ridge above Mongolia and China bowls, eventually reaching Vail's Two Elk Lodge, so stay high as you traverse toward the ski area boundary. Aim to meet the road that meets the top of the Mongolia lift. Continue along this spectacular ridge, bypassing Two Elk Lodge at 11,220 feet.

U.S. Army Tenth Mountain Division skiing soldiers trained on the Commando Run. Minot "Minnie" Dole, founder of the U.S. National Ski Patrol had noted the success of Finnish ski troops in stalemating an early World War II Russian invasion. Dole spearheaded an American army ski unit. After Camp Hale (named for Brigadier General Irving Hale, a Denver West Pointer) sprang into being, the nation's top skiers, plus many foreign ski greats and a host of novices gathered there to train. They quickly learned that on high-altitude traverses like the Commando Run, 40-below temperatures made metal zippers stick, tearing flesh from frozen fingers. Tents collapsed under heavy snowfall. Eventually, improved clothing and equipment replaced old, and Arctic explorer Dr. Vilhjamer Stefansson arrived to teach troops to build snow caves.

The next part of the hike crisscrosses Vail Mountain's eastern flank. Gentle Vail Mountain, unlike its jagged neighbors, formed through erosion deposits from ancient mountains by an ancient sea. Take the Tin Pants ski run past the bottom of the Sourdough lift (chair 14) and continue on Flapjack to the clearing between the top of Riva Bahn and the bottom of Northwoods Express.

Please note: It's tempting to escape a thunderstorm by scurrying under the express lift's big station. Don't do this. The metal structures act as big conductors during electrical storms.

Pick up Mill Creek Road, using Brisk Walk and Brisk Way as shortcuts. Note the sign for Golden Peak, your destination, and turn onto the Golden Peak mountain bike race trail (unless a race is underway!) to return to your car.

Ski Touring/Snowshoeing (Most difficult): Aggressive winter trekkers with mountaineering skills can use this route. However, the 18-mile winter trail begins at the Vail Pass rest area where the marked Shrine Pass road, a snow-covered track, begins. Use directions for the Commando Run, page 120-121.

Skiers and snowshoers can choose to descend Vail Mountain on the ski runs used by hikers (see above) or they can follow the snowy 3.3 mile Mill Creek Road used by the technical Commando Run. Exercise extreme caution if you choose to plunge through Mushroom Bowl along this route as it is avalanche-prone. Turn off at Riva Bahn to reach the Golden Peak base.

Views, views, views, Commando Ridge has 'em. But also consider the trees here. High, dry slopes support the Englemann spruce and subalpine fir. The spruce has a square, pointed, sharp needle. The gray-barked fir has softer, flatter needles and its frozen cones disintegrate in winter, leaving only a stub.

Map printed from TOPO! National Geographic Holdings (www.topo.com)

45

14   SHRINE RIDGE

Time: 4-5 hours
Distance: 1.5 miles
Elevation gain: 937 feet
High point: 11,977 feet
Rating: Moderate
Usually open: July-September
Topo: USGS Vail Pass and USGS Red Cliff, 1987

For an eye-popping 360-degree view of Ten Mile, Sawatch, Flat Top and Gore Ranges, plus the mountains around Vail Pass, try this short hike to Shrine Ridge. The trail is easy except for the final climb to the ridge top, which gains almost 400 feet in less than 0.2 miles (something like climbing inside the Statue of Liberty). Wildlife abounds. The Utes hunted here for centuries. Excavation of stratified tribal campsites, carbon-dated back to 7,000 years ago, produced a wealth of arrowheads and hunting tools here during Vail Pass highway construction.

Drive to the Vail Pass I-70 summit and exit to the Shrine Pass dirt road, just west of the interchange. Follow this easy road 2.3 miles to just past the indistinct Shrine Pass summit and forest boundary. You will be able to see Shrine Ridge, your destination, above on your left. Park near a gravel driveway for the Shrine Mountain Inn. The trailhead is on the track to the left of the driveway.

The trail begins as an abandoned two-wheel road to the creek, which may be dry in late season. Beyond the creek, the track goes ahead left but your footpath goes right. Follow the foot trail as it climbs southwest through pine-studded meadow and up into dense forest.

After a mile or so, the trail enters a large, flat, green meadow at the valley's end. The trail tends to play tricks here because the wet meadow quickly overgrows it. However, the trail will climb the ridge on its north (right) shoulder. Look for the footpath snaking up the steep incline.

Take plenty of time to explore this "room at the top" near 12,000 feet. The full-circle of views includes:

North: The primitive 12,000-foot-plus Gore Range, 600 million-year-old Pre-Cambrian granite and gneiss (hikes 1-8). *Northwest:* The Corral Creek drainage and 12,522-foot Uneva Peak (hike no. 11). *Northeast:* The Vail Pass rest area and the historic red-dirt Shrine Pass Road. *East-southeast:* Copper Mountain Ski Area with its resort village below and the magnificent Ten Mile Range beyond. *South:* Ptarmigan Pass, 11,765 feet, route to biking, ski and hut trails, and Ptarmigan Hill, a rounded 12,143-foot bump above it (hike no. 15). *Southwest:* The Sawatch Range and Mount Holy Cross (hikes 16-19). *West:* The Flat Top Range in the far distance. *Northwest:* A man-shape rock we call "Lord Gore."

Named "Shrine" for its excellent view of the venerated Mount of the Holy Cross, the pass was temporarily called Holy Cross Trail in 1923. The route originated as a Ute Indian trail which came from Silver Plume over Loveland Pass, through the Ten Mile Canyon and across Shrine Pass. It once was a major Denver-Glenwood route. When the cry of "Silver!" brought miners to today's Red Cliff in 1879, the new town at the southern foot of Shrine Pass became Eagle County seat. The Denver & Rio Grande Railway arrived there in 1881 to serve a growing town with five hotels, three business offices and a brass band. A smelter and opera house came later. By 1884, Red Cliff had a population of 800, a thriving newspaper and a postoffice.

Ski Touring/Snowshoeing (Moderate): The 12-mile ski trip from the Vail Pass rest area to Red Cliff via the Shrine Pass Road offers an easy climb to a 11,050-foot summit and then a long, sweet drop to Red Cliff at 8,630 feet. (Check signs for skier-only routes.) Plan 6-7 hours on skis, plus time to leave a second car in Red Cliff. (It's 30 miles from the trailhead by car to Red Cliff.)

The trail provides some nice glissades and schusses as it rolls downhill on a clear route to Red Cliff. During mid-winter, the final 1.2 miles into town is skiable, despite plowing, but after mid-March, plan on walking.

Snowshoers can choose a destination a short distance beyond the Shrine Mountain Inn, a Tenth Mountain Trail System hut, to view the Sawatch Range.

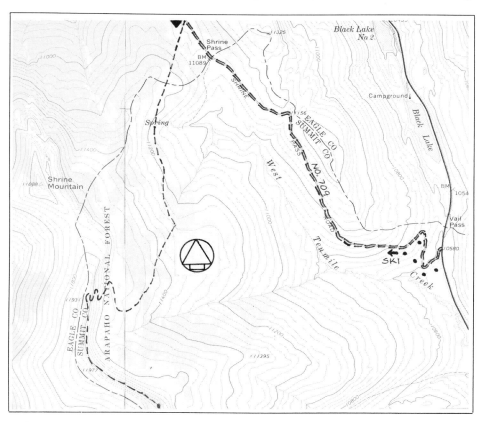

You can view Shrine Ridge from the road. A new trailhead with improved parking enhances a reconstructed trail. Heavy use here created side trails and wetland damage. Please help—stay on this delicate trail.

"Lord Gore"

15 WILDER GULCH

Time: 3 hours
Distance: 3.1 miles
Elevation gain: 1,365 feet
High point: 11,765 feet
Rating: Moderate
Usually open: July to September
Topo: USGS Vail Pass, 1987

July 15 to August 1 is peak wildflower time on Vail Pass. Both Shrine Pass above and Wilder Gulch just below offer sun-splashed meadows with many subalpine zone flowers. Look for larkspur, kittens paw, queens crown, Indian paintbrush and fields of mariposa lily. The hike to a green saddle called Ptarmigan Pass offers seclusion and beauty. Wilder Gulch is a good hike for families with kids beyond the "little" stage. Just be careful on the bike path.

Drive I-70 east to the Vail Pass summit, exit 190. Park in the roomy rest stop parking area. Geologists say that mountain passes began eons ago as faults or cracks which collected water, widened and created a high passage.

The trail begins on the Summit County side, 0.5 miles below via the paved Vail Pass bikepath. Go south through the tunnel and, after passing a gray electrical box, right into Wilder Gulch's mouth. (Be wary of bikers.)

Hikers have, however, created an easier access. You can also get to to Wilder Gulch by traversing cross-country southwest from the Vail Pass rest stop. Look for the trail rising from the south end of the car park; it's shown as the skier's route on the map at right. Stay high to avoid the abundant willow patches. The trail drops later to meet the established gulch footpath.

Hike an old road uphill on the north-northwest creek bank (right side) along a meadow. When the trail forks, use the upper branch. It affords better views of the spectacular Ten Mile Range and avoids a serious bog on the lower trail. The track stays in the meadow for two-thirds of the hike, then enters conifer forest. Curving through trees, the path heads up an old telephone line cut, first moderately, then in a steep climb. Soon you emerge from the trees to view Ptarmigan Hill, a 12,143-foot bump, and Ptarmigan Pass, 11,765 feet.

A dirt road winds to the summit. Ptarmigan Pass offers great views of the Sawatch Range and the jagged Gore Range-Eagles Nest Wilderness north-northeast. Ptarmigan Hill at right is a fun climb for those with extra energy. It's 0.5 miles and 400 feet elevation gain for a great view. Be sure to choose your route downhill carefully—a very steep slope here presents some slippery scree.

Ski Touring/Snowshoeing (Moderate): Snowshoe or ski from the slope above the Vail Pass parking area south over open meadow to Wilder Gulch, the first drainage. You may encounter a snocat trail created by Resolution Snotours, a Vail Associates operation. The groomed path may help trail-breaking after a heavy snow. Snowmobiles also use Wilder Gulch, but the valley is big enough to accommodate mixed use.

Use the hikers' route up through the spruce forest but do not continue into the open snowfields near the Ptarmigan Pass unless snow is extremely stable. A long, sweet drop returns you to the valley's mouth where you veer left for the gentle climb to the Vail Pass summit.

Advanced skiers with expert ski skills can use Wilder Gulch to begin a 10.9 mile trip to Red Cliff on a low avalanche day. Make sure the snowpack is stable. Watch carefully for a fork to the right in an open area. Take it, cross the ridge then use Wearyman and Turkey Creeks to Red Cliff, an 1879 silver town.

48

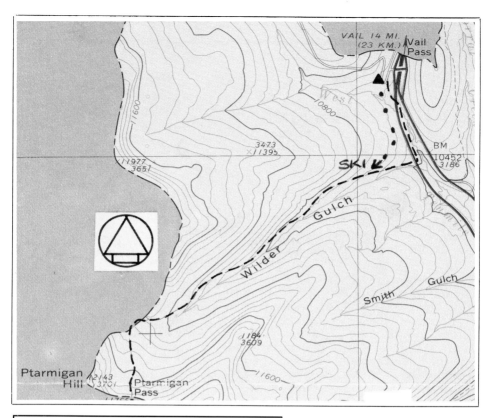

During a moist August, pine forests like those in Wilder Gulch produce wild mushrooms in abundance. Here, a cauliflower-like mushroom in the Ramaria family displays branchlets in sunny yellow.

16   HALF MOON PASS TRAIL/
MOUNT OF THE HOLY CROSS

Time: 4 hours
Distance: 3 miles
Elevation gain: 1,580 feet
High point: 11,900 feet
Rating: More difficult
Usually open: July-September
Topo: USGS Mount of the Holy Cross, 1987

Rich rewards await hikers who make the short but stiff climb to Half Moon Pass and beyond to the easy west slope of Notch Mountain. A dizzying variety of Gore and Mosquito Range views present themselves at the Pass. Then an up-close view of the Mount of the Holy Cross appears from Notch, along with staggering views of the 13,000-foot Holy Cross Ridge. Finally, a panorama of peaks marches across toward dramatic 13,670-foot Mount Jackson.

Drive 5 miles south of I-70 exit 171 to the Tigiwon Road, no 707. Turn right just before the Eagle River and proceed 8.5 miles on a road that can be rough or moderate depending on when it was last graded. At 1.7 miles, note the Cross Creek trailhead (hike no. 20). Pass the Tigiwon Community House at 6 miles. Built in the 1930s to shelter groups of Christians making the Mount of the Holy Cross pilgrimage, the Tigiwon House is named with a Ute Indian word meaning "friends." Look for wildlife along this trail in summer; snowmobiles drive the animals away in winter. A generous parking area at road's end provides staging space for two trailheads here: The Fall Creek Trail, used for both Lake Constantine and Notch Mountain; and the Half Moon Pass trailhead. Hikers seeking to climb the Mount of the Holy Cross, a two-day trip, also use Half Moon, so plan on plenty of people weekends and holidays. (The Forest Service may charge a use fee in future seasons.)

The trail, an old stock path, climbs without mercy up the rocky 2-mile route to the pass. You emerge from trees at 1.2 miles to confront the first of the trail's staggering views, a Gore Range vista north to northeast and the Mosquito Range southeast. Flowers abound. The Half Moon Pass summit at 11,600 feet is a narrow footpath through rubble rock alive with the colors of green lichen on pink and black dappled rock. The East Cross Creek valley, punctuated by ponds, lies below. Notch Mountain is just south (left).

East Cross Creek, which flows from the famous Bowl of Tears beneath the Mount, frustrated early artist Thomas Moran. His effort to approach the peak to paint it was hampered by the valley's 3-4-foot deep fallen burnt logs and huge rounded rocks.

Holy Cross View: Continue on the trail over the pass and descend into a grove of subalpine fir. Traverse a talus slope. Now, follow these directions carefully. About 0.3 miles from the pass, just beyond the talus rock and about 200 yards beyond the end of the woods, look for several snags (weathered still-standing dead trees) a few on the left and a few on the right. Leave the footpath here. Turn left and climb a flower-carpeted tundra slope. Brilliant red, orange and gold in September, it displayed several varieties of mountain gentian. Go uphill, staying just high enough to be above the trees. Soon the pyramid-shaped Mount comes into view. The wild stretch of 13,000-foot Holy Cross ridge coming from the south ends at the Mount of the Holy Cross.

Look for a huge and unmistakable rock outcropping ahead on the grassy Notch Mountain slope. Travel to just above or below the rock and continue beyond at the same elevation for a smashing Holy Cross view. The final viewpoint lies at a cluster of boulders. Beyond that, travel becomes difficult.

Mount of the Holy Cross Climb: The snow-filled crevasse on the mount's northeast flank lies below the climbing route up its obvious north-facing ridge. Hikers cross Half Moon Pass, drop to the East Cross Creek valley and pick up a 2.5 mile trail across the creek that follows this north flank up through boulders to the summit. Due to frequent afternoon electrical storms on the mountain, many climbers overnight on Cross Creek and complete the ascent before noon the next day. Leave no trace—this area suffers overuse.

Ski Touring/Snowshoeing (Moderate): Nova Guides has a use permit to conduct snowmobile tours on the Tigiwon Road. You can ski alongside snowmobiles for a day tour; use the snowy road for a quiet moonlight tour; or call Nova Guides at 827-4232 for a snowmobile ride to the Tigiwon Community House (or Half Moon) for a reasonable fee. Then you can snowshoe or ski from Tigiwon to Half Moon or tour terrain surrounding Half Moon.

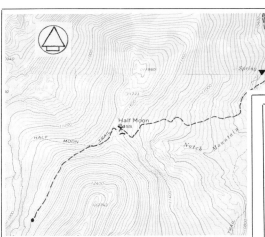

A multitude of mountains creates a dramatic vista from soaring Half Moon Pass and the Notch Mountain view-point at trail's end.

Hikers leave the Half Moon trail to traverse Notch Mountain slope for a special view.

Time: 6-8 hours
Distance: 5 miles
Elevation gain: 2,780 feet
High point: 13,100 feet
Rating: More difficult
Usually open: July-September
Topo: USGS Mount of the Holy Cross, 1987

Rumors of a cross of snow on a mountain in Colorado's rugged Rockies persisted until 1869 when William Brewer and his party sighted the fabled Holy Cross from Grays Peak near today's Loveland Pass.

The American spirit, deeply rooted in Christianity, stirred to this newly-revealed symbol of faith. On August 23, 1873 William Henry Jackson, Hayden survey party photographer, made the first glass plate negative of the elusive cross. Jackson had promised his finacee, Emilie Painter, that he would locate (if it existed) the elusive Holy Cross and photograph it for her as a wedding gift. He did and they were married October 8, 1873.

His photographs circulated, prompting national veneration of the mount. Later in 1922, the government dedicated a shrine on Shrine Pass and in 1929 created the now-defunct Holy Cross National Monument. Pilgrims streamed up Notch Mountain to a flat, rock-strewn meadow above 13,000 feet where the Holy Cross stands smack in front of hikers, just across a narrow, deep chasm.

That stunning view is the reason for this climb. Go in early July to see snow in the cross.

Drive 5 miles south on U.S. 24 from I-70 exit 171 to Tigiwon Road, no. 707. Turn right and proceed 8.5 miles to the trailhead at road's end. Road conditions vary from rough to acceptable, depending on when grading last occurred. Park and find the marked trailhead at left.

The trail penetrates a thick, cool pine forest, which soon opens across a meadow to provide a view of Notch Mountain, your destination. Notice the significant notch for which the peak is named. Later, you'll pass by the notch at much closer range.

After a vigorous climb, the trail curves around a steep valley wall. The first of many spectacular views begins here with the massive Ten Mile Range east. After more woods, a small stream and a scree patch, meet the junction of two trails, one southwest to beautiful Lake Constantine, the other west to Notch Mountain. A sign marks this fork at 2 miles. Turn right for Notch Mountain.

Now the climb begins. But so do the views. As the trees clear, look northeast to spot Gilman, an 1879-founded silver town on the slopes of Battle Mountain. Gilman, with a 300 population in 1899, suffered a disastrous fire that year which wiped out the Iron Mask Hotel, the schoolhouse, stores, restaurants and the big Bell Mine's shaft house and machinery. But the company town, now closed, grew to 8,970 in 1960 when the Empire Zinc Company of New Jersey operated mines there.

At 3 miles, start the series of above-timberline switchbacks (we counted 36) that get increasingly tighter as they approach the summit. Steepness and a rocky trail pale in comparison to the sweeping vistas: The Gore; the Continental Divide peaks with Grays and Torreys, two famous 14ers; the craggy Ten Mile Range stretching south to Fremont Pass; the Mosquito Range; Robinson Lake, a Climax Mine tailings site; the Resolution Creek Road; and Ski Cooper. Glimpse the sapphire shimmer of three unnamed tarns below, then

Lake Constantine nestled against Mount Whitney.

Emerge at the summit meadow to find a stone hut built in 1924 to shelter Holy Cross pilgrims. Two hundred Civilian Conservation Corps workers built the house at a cost of $120,000. It's difficult to imagine how materials for this roomy shelter arrived. But a poured concrete floor, a large rock fireplace with mantle and three-part paneled windows show evidence of great effort. Across the deep cleft between Notch and the 14,006-foot Mount of the Holy Cross stands the 1,500-foot high cross, with its horizontal arms stretching almost 750 feet on each side.

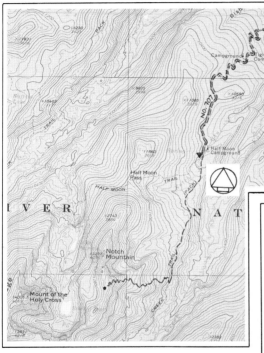

Sapphire tarns glisten below Notch Mountain trail where knockout views to surrounding mountain valleys and ranges continually appear.

Mount of the Holy Cross, photographed from Notch Mountain in early October during a snow-free autumn, displays ravines 50-80 feet deep that hold tons of winter snow.

18   LAKE CONSTANTINE

Time: 5-6 hours
Distance: 3.5 miles
Elevation gain: 1,120 feet
High point: 11,440 feet
Rating: Moderate
Usually open: July-September
Topo: USGS Mount of the Holy Cross, 1987

Set in the wildflower-pocketed Fall Creek valley, Lake Constantine shines like a gem in its rich mounting. Natural beauty on both sides of 12,580-foot Fall Creek Pass is unsurpassed. You can drink in this beauty on a moderate hike to a pristine lake where large smooth shoreline rocks invite picnicking. Those desiring a longer hike can continue to the pass, another 1.5 miles, where long views to 14,265-foot Gray's Peak far away east on the Continental Divide and short views to the Seven Sisters Lakes below will reward hikers.

Drive U.S. 24 5 miles south of I-70 exit 171 to the Tigiwon Road, no. 707. Turn right and proceed a bumpy 8.5 miles to the trailhead at road's end. You will pass the Cross Creek trailhead (hike no. 20) at 1.7 miles and the Tigiwon Community House at 6 miles. Arrive early to park and find the trailhead at left (south). Another trailhead here at west provides access to Half Moon Pass and a close-up Holy Cross view (hike no. 16).

The trail penetrates a dark, cool pine forest on a wide, smooth path. An opening in the trees offers a view across a meadow to 13,237-foot Notch Mountain, named for a large notch north of its summit. You'll climb on an irregular but always moderate grade along a broad slope to arrive at a steep valley above the beaver-pond-dotted Fall Creek drainage. The trail hugs a sheer-drop hillside here affording views east to the towering Ten Mile Range.

At 2 miles, the footpath forks, with the right branch heading west to climb Notch Mountain. The Lake Constantine trail continues straight ahead (left) on a southwesterly tack. Soon, wet meadows appear, a riot of colorful beauty in July. The subalpine flowers that bloom in wet conditions seem to be the brightest in hue. Little red elephant, pink and red paintbrush, rosy queens crown and many more stand out against the green meadows.

The lake lies below a low shoulder of 13,271-foot Whitney Peak. Shaped a bit like a boomerang, Lake Constantine curves around to the southwest in a large clear-water expanse. Please protect this fragile alpine area. The Minturn Ranger District says this Holy Cross Wilderness lake has suffered "high resource damage."

Tigiwon, a Ute Indian word, means friends. The Utes frequented this area before their deportation to reservations in 1879-81. Nearby Battle Mountain, 10,956 zinc-rich feet, is named for a fierce Ute-Arapahoe battle in 1849. The Utes made ferocious enemies for the Cheyenne and Arapahoe but they welcomed miners and trappers. When prospectors pushed over Tennessee Pass to discover silver near Red Cliff and Gilman in 1879, the clash between Ute land use and acreage-hungry farmers had already forced the Utes from their mountain homeland. By the time the Rio Grande railway rumbled along the Eagle River valley past Red Cliff, Belden, Astor City and Gilman to reach the Minturn lumber/rail center in 1887, the Utes were long gone.

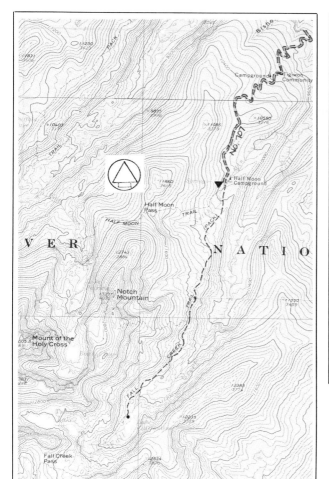

Watch for wildlife on Tigiwon Road. Deer a- bound in summer. A short hike beyond Lake Constan- tine toward Fall Creek Pass yields views east to the Continental Divide near Eisenhower Tunnel with towering 14ers, Grays and Torreys Peaks, rising above all.

19   TUHARE LAKES

Time: 6-7 hours
Distance: 5 miles
Elevation gain: 2,045 feet
High point: 12,365 feet
Rating: More difficult
Usually open: July-September
Topo: USGS Mount of the Holy Cross

The flower-crammed coloirs, gullies and gorges of a wild basin below Fall Creek Pass reward hikers with the best of the Holy Cross Wilderness. Of course, you earn the reward. A long, bumpy ride to the trailhead and a steep scramble to reach the Tuhare Lakes are the price. Green subalpine meadows rioting red paintbrush, pink sticky geranium and yellow groundsel are one reward. Another is the boulder-dominated Lower Tuhare Lake. Add to that a stunning waterfall and a 13,000-foot razorback called Holy Cross Ridge.

Do take the camera but don't take the kids. Wear boots with an excellent tread. And avoid this challenging trail in the rain.

Drive using directions for hike no. 18, Lake Constantine. Due to limited parking, choose this trail mid-week, if possible.

The trail follows the path to Lake Constantine, described in hike no. 18. The unparalleled beauty of this wilderness hike has prompted visitors to "love it to death." Hikers should stay on the one established trail, even where it crosses a big rock, to protect this fragile treasure.

The Tuhare Lakes lie 1.5 miles west of Lake Constantine. Hikers gain most of the 1,000 foot altitude gain on the trail above Constantine in the final two-thirds of the climb.

Leaving Lake Constantine, follow the continuing trail southwest through one of Colorado's prime wildflower gardens. If you go in July, you'll see masses of columbine niched in the rock; pockets of purple penstamen, heavy with blossom clusters; and slopes mantled by purple fleabane, scarlet paintbrush and white American bistort. Blue chimingbells, pink Parry's primrose and white brook cress crowd streamsides.

When you reach the junction, go right for Tuhare Lakes. (The left fork continues to Fall Creek Pass.) Now the climb steepens.

Lower Tuhare Lake lies about 45 minutes hiking time above Constantine. After scaling a short cliff-like trail section, hikers arrive on a green table at 11,800 feet. Look left here for a small tarn. Then the trail maintains its sharp ascent to the breathtaking Lower Tuhare Lake. The lung-expanding climb takes place alongside a waterfall guaranteed to take more of your breath away! First a crystal spurt, the cascade widens to a shining sheet which flows across a large, flat rectangular rock face. As you traverse higher on the rubble rock trail, the falls transmutes into multiple cascades, crisscrossing in a mad tumble.

Room-size boulders lodged in its serene waters render Lower Tuhare Lake at 12,090 feet unique. A rock wall displaying yet another waterfall (ho hum) dominates the lake's western shore.

To reach Upper Tuhare, continue west around the lower lake, crossing rocks where the trail fades, to a saddle. Below you, glacier-sculpted into a gentler bowl, lies 12,365-foot Upper Tuhare Lake. Beyond rises the Holy Cross ridge, jag-toothed and splendid.

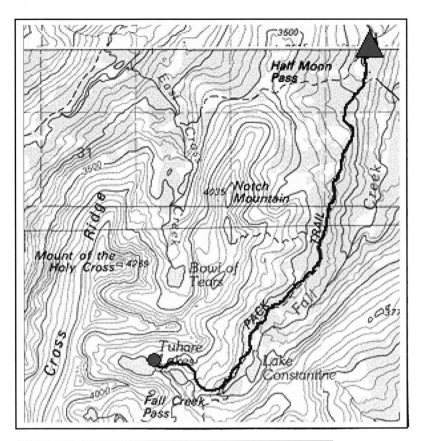

Take time to relax at Tuhare Lakes. Take time also to listen for the whistle pig, the fat and friendly marmot. He "pigs out" in summer to prepare to hibernate. His temperature falls to 45 degrees and pulse to 3-10 beats per minute. But intense cold triggers an alarm waking him before he freezes.

Map reprinted from TOPO! National Geographic Holdings (www.topo.com)

Kids' Hike to Bridge:

Time: 5-6 hours
Distance: 5.5 miles
Elevation gain: 1,080 feet
High point: 9,600 feet
Rating: Easy
Usually open: June-September
Topo: USGS Minturn, 1987

Time: 2-3 hours
Distance: 1 mile
Elevation gain: 200 feet
High point: 8,700 feet
Rating: Easy
Usually open: June-September

Backpackers love Cross Creek because the long route offers nearly 20 miles of scenic terrain without the taxing climbs required by many high-country trails. Reeds Meadow, a knockout glacial valley at 7 miles makes a good first night destination for backpackers. This hike, a berrypickers' special, goes to a meandering meadow at 5.5 miles. The trail's first bridge, with picnic/play rocks surrounding it, makes a good destination for a hike with kids.

Drive 5 miles south on U.S. 24 from I-70 Dowd Junction exit 171 to the Tigiwon Road, no. 707. Turn right and proceed 1.7 miles to the trailhead.

The trail winds and undulates through deep forest along the southeast bank of Cross Creek, then drops at 1.0 mile to a meadow and bridge across the wide creek, a good destination for **the Kids' Hike.** Climb the opposite bank to hike in more open terrain. Bring a container in late July for thimbleberries, the edible red raspberry-like fruit with a broad five-point leaf. They're thicker here than any trailside location around.

Two trail forks may now present problems. The initial one is just beyond the first of several mammoth rocks at trail left. Avoid a tread that goes downhill right. Just beyond, a marshy pond appears at about 2 miles. Past this pond lies a turn in the trail where many hikers go wrong. (A myriad of false trails on the hillside above evidences this error.) Beyond the marshy pond the trail dissolves on a bare, pine needle-littered forest floor beneath huge conifers. The trail appears to go uphill right and curve around a small side stream. This is the wrong way. Instead, enter the shady conifers to pick up the trail.

Note the house-size rocks that begin to rise along the path.

Opening up among clustered aspen-pine groves, the trail crosses a stream and stays within listening distance of Cross Creek. Later, the footpath follows the bottom of a crevasse which is walled on the left by a huge rock formation. Cliffs above intrigue rock lovers. After another giant stone block at left, watch for a little trail heading uphill left where you can climb the ridge for a view of Cross Creek, a deep plunge below. Returning to the main route, continue to the third stream crossing, over a log bridge. The fourth ford crosses over rocks. Then the trail forks at the meadow, this hike's destination. The left fork goes to campsites and a nice meadow view spot. Cross Creek, more a river than a creek, flows across the meadow left. It is known for good fishing. A bridge at right crosses the stream to continue the main trail.

The Cross Creek Trail, following the southwest bank of the main creek, continues. It meets the Grouse Mountain Trail junction at 6 miles, scenic Reeds Meadow at 7 miles, then traverses the eastern flank of Middle Mountain to Harvey Lake at about 11 miles. The trail passes Blodgett and Treasure Vault Lakes in a climb to either Fancy or Missouri Pass and a downhill walk to the Gold Park/Homestead area.

Fairly level Cross Creek footpath offers Notch Mountain view near trailhead, then constant glimpses of the Mount of the Holy Cross. The Forest Service allows no horse use.

Backpackers on 20 mile Cross Creek Trail rest in woods just below the meadow at 5.5 miles that makes this hike's destination.

21   GROUSE LAKE

Time: 5-6 hours
Distance: 6.25 miles
Elevation gain: 2,840 feet
High point: 10,680 feet
Rating: More difficult
Usually open: June-September
Topo: USGS Minturn, 1987

Grouse Lake, balmy, serene and known for fine fishing, provides a good spot to relax after an aerobic walk up the trail. This shallow, rock-studded lake rests beneath massive 12,799-foot Grouse Mountain. A good hike for a hot day, the climb is cooled by mossy forest and six stream crossings enroute.

Drive 1.6 miles south on U.S. 24 from I-70 exit 171 at Dowd Junction. The trailhead, marked with signs and fenced parking, is on the road's south side.

The trail follows a dirt road south of the trailhead 0.75 miles to a footpath. The dry hillside here blooms with sage and miners candle. Both the Grouse Creek Trail and the shorter trail to Grouse Lake begin here on this path. Soon a fork appears. The Grouse Lake route goes left. The trail rises through aspen, pine, spruce and fir, with lupine thick beneath the trees. Near 1.2 miles, cross Grouse Creek on two logs and begin a climb. All the steeper sections on the trail are short, so hikers can catch their breath on the flats. Cross water six times, including an irrigation canal once used to irrigate nearby hay meadows, such as Meadow Mountain. Look for water-loving wildflowers at stream crossings, including white brook cress. Later, a series of meadows interrupt the woods. Look for larkspur, monks hood, western paintbrush, senecio, wild geranium, harebell, fireweed and aspen daisy in mid-summer. In late summer, purple gentian and star gentian bloom here, with mushrooms in the cool woods. Views from these upper meadows soar east to the Gore Range.

A final climb brings you into the Holy Cross Wilderness and to Grouse Lake, the shallow pine-rimmed habitat of the wily brook trout. The lake is alive with jumping fish. A marsh stretches beyond Grouse Lake toward the foot of domineering Grouse Mountain. Explore the rock field just west of the lake for its room-size boulders.

Grouse Lake, Creek and Mountain bear the name of the slow-moving (and slow-witted) grouse or ptarmigan, a large, gentle bird that turns from brown in summer to snow white in winter. Plentiful in this area, the grouse is often seen marching a string of babies across the hiking trail. Local lore says that mama grouse will not run away unless you look straight at her, as a predator would. If you watch her from the corner of your eye, she's fooled. Try it!

Usually meek and defenseless, the mother grouse can demonstrate fearless resolve when her chicks face danger. Our group stumbled upon a mom with seven chicks who, seeing no escape route, raised her wings menacingly and advanced upon us in a ferocious attack mode. We gave her a wide berth—and hats off for courage.

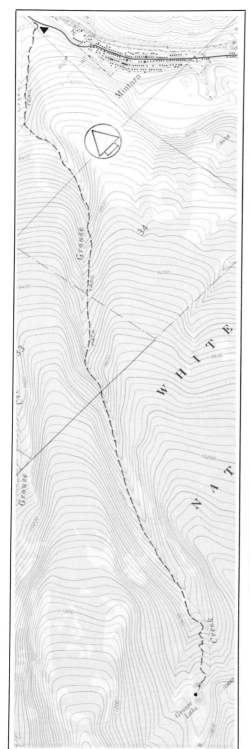

Try fishing Grouse Lake, guarded here by its sentinel, towering Grouse Mountain. Hikers will climb through conifers to get here with a few views but lots of pine-scented woodland glades and flora of the shady forest floor, as seen below.

22   WEST GROUSE CREEK
To Olsen Lake

Time: 6-7 hours
Distance: 6 miles
Elevation gain: 2,960 feet
High point: 10,800 feet
Rating: More difficult
Usually open: Mid-June-September
Topo: USGS Minturn, 1987 and USGS Grouse Mountain, 1987

A nice workout with a sweet destination—that sums up the day hike along West Grouse Creek to Olsen Lake. Nearly 3,000 feet in elevation gain provides the workout; an iridescent lake is the reward. For backpackers, the trail opens an array of longer hiking experiences: You can continue to Turquoise Lakes at trail's end (10 miles) and return via Beaver Creek to Avon. You can connect to the little-used Grouse Mountain Trail and visit Buffalo Lake, a good place to spot wildlife, then hike out via Cross Creek.

Drive 1.6 miles south on U.S. 24 from I-70 exit 171 at Dowd Junction. The trailhead, marked with Forest Service sign and fenced parking, is on the highway's south side.

The trail follows a dirt road south of the trailhead up 0.75 miles to a footpath. Sage and miners candle cover the dry hillside. Both the West Grouse Creek and the Grouse Lake trails begin on this footpath. Soon a fork appears; go right for West Grouse Creek.

First aspen, then spruce, pine and fir comprise the forest that dominates this trail. Cross a logging road and continue on the footpath. Raspberries and their thorn-free look-alike, the edible thimbleberries, grow here. Despite the nearly 3,000-foot altitude gain, the trail itself is in good shape. Many long smooth stretches make the unyielding climb enjoyable.

Cross the creek on a nice log bridge. Huge rounded boulders protrude from the creek here. Five ruined cabins and scattered remains of an old stove lie beside West Grouse Creek above the bridge. The trail climbs continuously. Though it passes Waterdog Lake, the lake is not visible from the path. At the intersection with the short Olsen Lake path, swing north for a less than half-mile trip to the lake. A massive ridge rises from Olsen Lake, dominating the scene. The ridge separates West Grouse from the Beaver Creek drainage. Trees rim the lake on two-thirds of its shoreline.

Ski Touring/Snowshoeing (More difficult): Trek up the hiking trail to the logging road that bisects the route then cut across to Meadow Mountain. Skiers get a thrilling downhill schuss over rolling hills. Try it on a fresh-snow morning and float over acres of powder on a gentle drop to Meadow Mountain's base. Snowshoers love the open expanse of white.

Drive 0.4 miles south of I-70 to the Forest Service parking at Meadow Mountain's base. Park. Drive a second car 0.8 miles ahead at the Grouse Creek trailhead. When the snow is deep, you can ski to the trail start.

Using the hiking trailhead, proceed just south of the fenced summer parking (often unplowed during winter) and curve around a side hill where the snow-covered road climbs southwest. Ascend on the road to the signed footpath. Tree blazes also mark the route. When the trail forks, stay right. The route is not difficult to follow. It stays left of the creek, which flows below in a deep ravine. The trail stays fairly close to the bank. Note the ridge across the creek. It will remain steep until you approach the junction with the logging road. Then the ridge softens and the gulch ahead closes up. The creek, well below all along, becomes nearly level with the trail. Watch carefully here for the snow-obliterated road.

Turn right onto the road, which is level at first then switchbacks left in a climb. Soon you find yourself on the old Meadow Mountain Ski Area runs. A pleasant drop to the base parking area provides a fine finish to the tour.

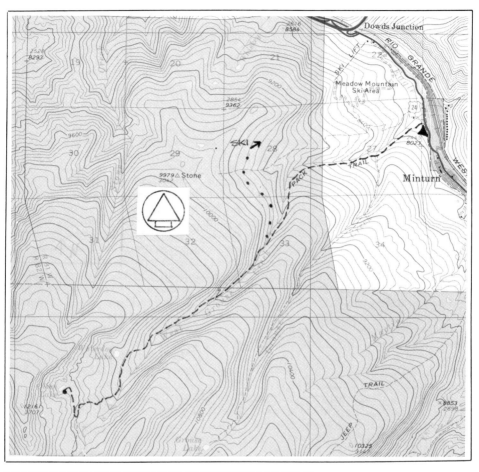

Although scenic Olson Lake lies within Holy Cross Wilderness boundaries, most of the trail does not. The path is well maintained, unlike some Wilderness trails that are allowed to erode to preserve their "primitive" character.

23   MEADOW MOUNTAIN

Time: 4-5 hours
Distance: 3.5 miles
Elevation gain: 1,920 feet
High point: 9,760 feet
Rating: Moderate
Usually open: June-September
Topo: USGS Minturn, 1987 or: USGS Eagle County, 1975, Sheet 4

Hikers, mountain bikers, cross-country skiers and snowshoers love Meadow Mountain for its gentle terrain and mellow beauty. Pastoral in summer with its aging ranch structures and wildflowers, Meadow Mountain becomes a winter recreationists' dream. Pick a powder day and get there early to beat the snowmobiles. A shelter at 3.5 miles makes a good destination.

Drive 0.4 miles south from I-70 Dowd Junction exit 171 to the U.S. Forest Service Minturn Ranger Station and park.

The trail begins at the parking lot's south end on a closed road that once served the early 1970s ski area here for lift construction and maintenance.

The route, which is road all the way to the rustic shelter at top, switchbacks in a southwesterly direction up into the sloping ranchlands. Meadow Mountain stands as a symbol of Eagle County's rich ranching history. From here to Eagle, with the Vail valley included, 1800s pioneers homesteaded 160-acre parcels, raising sheep, cattle, hay and at one time, an abundance of crisp mountain lettuce. Never rich but blessed nevertheless, they dined on wild raspberries and fresh cream in summer and game in winter. They sent their children to log schoolhouses, fished the trout streams and explored the wild mountain country on horseback. They stocked firewood and supplies each September and endured the long snowbound winters dreaming of spring.

Rising above the lower ranchlands, the trail begins to offer long views. Hikers can see into the Game Creek drainage to the east and later into Vail's green Game Creek ski bowl above. Reach a fork in the trail and stay straight ahead (right). The left fork leads to a devastated logging area and also intersects the West Grouse Creek Trail (no. 22).

After the fork, the trail moves from aspen into conifers, broken by big open meadows. The trail continues to switchback, opening up views northeast to the Gore Range and its primitive Eagles Nest Wilderness (trails no. 1-8). Ski runs of the Beaver Creek Ski Area appear west as do great views of the Vail Ski Mountain back side. Serenity reigns on these breeze-swept high meadows.

The one-room cabin at 9,760 feet once nicely outfitted with bed, table and chairs, has gone downhill. Though hikers share this trail with mountain bikers, its width accommodates both. Nor does this non-motorized use drive away the deer. Hikers can continue above the line shack for glad-to-be-alive views.

Ski Touring/Snowshoeing (Moderate): Snowshoers abound on Meadow Mountain. The easy road begins as described in the hiking directions. Wind protective clothing is suggested due to the open nature of the trail. An exposed ridge at 2 miles is often wind-blown, with hard-packed snow. If you lose the trail be aware that it climbs generally west-southwest. The cabin at 3.5 miles makes a good lunch stop and provides sweeping views. Please respect cabin property and rights of others at this shelter.

Novice skiers and snowshoers may choose to follow the road down. Advanced recreationists will enjoy the freedom of open meadows and the challenging steeper runs funneling to the base.

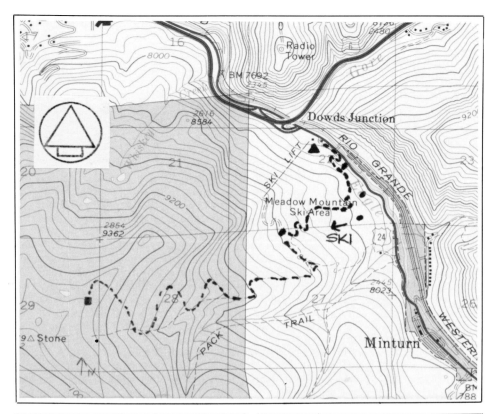

Nothing is sweeter for skiers on a fresh-snow morning than Meadow Mountain.

Originally the Nelson homestead, this mountain was purchased by Jack Oleson and developed as a ski area.

Time: 5 hours
Distance: 3.4 miles to meadow; 3.9 miles to Eagles Nest
Elevation gain: 2,350 feet
High point: 10,350 feet
Rating: More difficult
Usually open: June-September
Topo: USGS Minturn

When you want to leave the world behind (but not for long) retreat into the leafy sanctuary along the Game Creek Trail. Its quick access from Vail, Minturn, Eagle-Vail and Avon make Game Creek a hideaway for hikers who can't spend all day. Its rushing stream, lush vegetation and namesake wildlife make Game Creek's deep valley rich in dividends.

Drive I-70 to Dowd Junction, exit 171, and take U.S. 24 to Minturn's west entrance. (As you drive, look for Lions Head, a buff-colored rock outcropping 2,000 feet above the highway.) Enter Minturn and immediately turn left, crossing the bridge over the Eagle river and then curve around the brick building at right. Continue north on Minturn Road .04 mile, then turn right onto 4th Avenue. Then go left on North Taylor Street. Just .01 mile beyond lies the parking area for the Game Creek trailhead where you will begin. Walk uphill to the trailhead.

Option 1: **The trail** abruptly exits the real world to enter a creek canyon worlds away. Hikers pass private property and the turnoff at 0.5 miles for Lions Head (trail no. 25). The footpath continues along the creek, offering several places to picnic or refresh your feet in the icy water. The valley remains tight, with conifer forest on one side and aspen groves interrupted by sweet meadows on the other.

Wildflowers, including plentiful delphinium, line the trail. Look for bent grass, a green bamboo-like stalk, alongside the stream. More flowers crowd a side canyon at 1.5 miles (8,840 feet). It offers a refuge for solitude seekers.

Above, at 9,000 feet, the trail heads left to leave the creek, then switchbacks in a rousing climb to Eagles Nest. Hikers can make the view meadow at 10,200 feet their destination. (It's located just before the trail meets the ski area road system.) Or, they can continue to Eagles Nest, another 0.5 miles.

Energetic hikers with shuttle transportation can hike the Berrypicker trail down to Vail Village. Otherwise, return to the Game Creek trailhead.

Option 2: The trail can be reversed for less aggressive hikers. Walk it downhill. Leave a car at the Game Creek trailhead and then travel to Lionshead in a second vehicle. Park in the public parking structure (free in summer), and ride the Eagle Bahn gondola to Eagles Nest. Stop at the viewing platform for an eye-popping view of the Sawatch Range. Then pick up Eagles Loop trail to the road descending the valley. (Avoid the road leading to Chair 7; this is the wrong way.) Where the dirt road passes a grassy meadow, look for the footpath and turn onto it. Later meet a trail fork. A well-traveled path goes right. Choose the less-used left fork which will take you to Game Creek.

A large ice house once dominated the mouth of the Game Creek drainage. The fields above on the Nelson brothers' ranch (today's Meadow Mountain) produced acres of lettuce. Migrant Japanese workers harvested it, and ice from the Game Creek ice house kept the lettuce cool for transport on the railroad. In the 1920s and 30s, when mining had played out, farmers all over the high country grew lettuce, a good cash crop in tough economic times. Failure to rotate the crop eventually ruined the lettuce fields and the advent of the refrigerated rail car rendered the ice house obsolete.

Hiker at right cools his feet in glistening Game Creek. Below, a family chooses the easy downhill route from Vail Mountain.
Map reprinted from TOPO! National Geographic Holdings (www.topo.com)

Time: 2-3 hours
Distance: 2.2 miles
Elevation gain: 2,068 feet
High point: 9,928 feet
Rating: More difficult
Usually open: June-October
Topo: USGS Minturn

A quick trip that provides both an invigorating workout and the reward of sweeping views is something to roar about. Lions Head delivers, with a steep but easy-to-follow trail that pops hikers out of thick pine forest into a knockout panorama. The vista rises from the Eagle River valley up to rolling Meadow Mountain and skyward to the Grouse, Beaver Creek and Sawatch Range mountains.

Drive using directions for Game Creek, no. 24.

The trail rises sharply, then moderates, climbing into a leafy crevasse of aspen woods. Pass private property (please respect) and arrive quickly at the junction for the Lions Head trail at 0.5 miles. Go right.

Your climb takes you through a moist area where mountain bikers have damaged the trail in attempts to navigate the wetland. Soon the old roadway steepens but August hikers will find red raspberry-like thimbleberries to sample during rest stops. The aspen trees break to tantalize with big views from the cliffside. Look for the Grouse Creek and Meadow Mountain trails, numbers 22 and 23 in this book.

The ascent remains unyielding, however icy shadows in the pines provide relief. A breakout frames another splendid view. But where is the Lions Head?

Finally, an open flat area leads to the king-of-the-beasts vista from a tawny rock outcropping shaped like a lion's head.

Swivel your neck to take in views from the Tigiwon and Two Elk area at left to Eagle Vail and Avon beyond on the right. Look for the Mount of the Holy Cross and Notch Mountain in the middle. But avoid gaping at the view long enough to check out the small cleft in the rock beneath your feet. It's big enough to stumble on and deep enough to lose your mini-camera in forever.

Aggressive hikers who have arranged transportation can continue past the Lions Head southeast along the Cougar Ridge mountain bike trail to connect into Vail's Sundown Bowl. From there, pick up the Grand traverse trail. A right fork goes to the Wildwood restaurant, a well-deserved rest stop.

This sedimentary rock replica of a lion's noggin, a local landmark, inspired Vail's developers in naming Lionshead ski runs like Simba, Safari, Born Free, Bwana, Cub's Way and Pride.

When you return to the trailhead, look for the concrete ruins of an old ice house nearby. It employed several men, plus teenagers during the busy time. In Minturn's early days, before refrigeration, a hefty block of ice rested in each home's wooden ice chest to cool milk, cream, butter and meats. Minturn's ice supply came from Pando, near Tennessee Pass. There a railroad contractor maintained a large, shallow pond. When the ice thickened to three feet, two-man teams hand-cut it into big blocks with ice saws. Then horse teams, equipped with chains, pulled the huge ice blocks onto cars of a special ice train. When the train stopped at ice houses along the Denver & Rio Grande track, children saw visions of homemade ice cream.

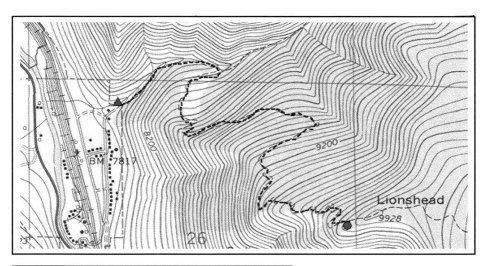

Looking south to the Two Elk valley from Lions Head Rock, the Minturn Formation cliffs command attention. Along the trail, sample thimbleberries in August. Similar to raspberries, without the thorn, they are soft and sweet when ripe. Hunt for chokecherries, a small dark purple-to-black berry, near the trailhead.

Map printed from TOPO! National Geographic Holdings (www.topo.com)

Time: 4-5 hours
Distance: 7.5 mile loop
Elevation gain: 2,120 feet
High point: 9,760 feet
Rating: **More** difficult
Usually open: July 1 to December 1 only
Topo: USGS Minturn

Glad-to-be alive views from upper Whiskey Creek Trail beat a day at the spa. Relics of the area's ranching past, such as homesteads, rail fences and corrals, resonate with history. You can go up the Whiskey Creek trail, then down Meadow Mountain to create a scenic horseshoe route.

Two cars are required if you choose the Meadow Mountain segment. Leave one car at Meadow Mountain using **Drive** directions for trail no. 23.

Drive a second car 1.4 miles to the Whiskey Creek trailhead on U.S. Hwy 6 southwest of Minturn. Proceed past the I-70 Dowd Junction exit 171 at 0.4 miles and continue another 1 mile to a concrete highway "box" underpass at left. Drivers, this is tricky to find for the first time. Traffic can be heavy, so be on guard. Look for the box on the left and a bus stop and parking area (six spaces) directly opposite on the right. Trailhead parking beyond the concrete underpass is best for high clearance vehicles.

The trail makes a lackluster start (just wait), beginning in a normally-muddy bog and continuing uphill on an inhospitable rocky track. Bush cover eliminates the possibility of views, which you suspect are smashing.

Then! Hikers emerge into the first of several meadows, complete with a rustic log homestead and mid-summer wildflowers. Settlers who first raised livestock and grew vegetables on these meadows arrived on the heels of the prospectors in the 1870s. After Eagle County split off from Summit County in 1883, Red Cliff mining created any news headlines the new area earned. The ranchers, often disgruntled former miners, created nostalgia rather than history. "Nuthin' went on here," one homesteader lamented. "We didn't even have a massacre."

As you cross the second meadow, be sure to take in the Gore Range/Eagles Nest views. Then enter a cool aspen forest, a haven for song birds. Later, trail spurs at left, right and again at left, remind hikers and bikers of trail responsibility. Stay on the main trail and avoid the "shortcut," especially the one heading straight up; it needs a chance to revegetate.

Emerge from another aspen glade to pass a charming zigzag fence on your approach to the hilltop.

Now expansive views sweep across green slopes to the rocky spires of the Gore Range. Pass a pond and then arrive at the Meadow Mountain line shack, a public-use cabin. Please respect this property. The Meadow Mountain summit provides views of Game Creek, Lions Head Rock (trails 24 and 25 in this book) as well as Vail Mountain.

Shepherds graze their flocks here. Give the sheep and dogs a wide berth.

The 1880 Red Cliff Comet reported on a St. Patrick's Day parade which also debuted the camp's new sawmill. The first log sawn, festooned in green boughs and pulled by a burro, led a parade of all the townsfolk. The marchers sang Irish melodies accompanied by a coronet. But the revelers' progress quickly diminished because they stopped at every saloon. Even the burro got drunk. Both man and beast staggered from too much of the libation for which

this trail is named: whiskey

Ski Touring/Snowshoeing (More difficult): Whiskey Creek Trail closes from December 1-July 1 for elk habitation and calving. Go early season or choose Meadow Mountain, a former downhill ski area. It offers perfect terrain for telemarkers, trail skiers and snowshoers. See directions for trail no. 23.

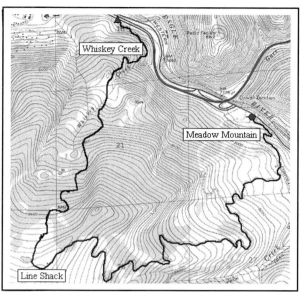

September color pleases walkers on the Whiskey Creek Trail. The trembling aspen (populus tremuloides) grows its leaf blade at a right angle to the spine of its stem, causing the leaf to quake in the slightest draft. The resulting rustle is a friendly sound to hikers
Map printed from TOPO! National Geographic Holdings (www.topo.com)

Trails near Homestake Reservoir

27 WHITNEY LAKE

Time: **4 hours**
Distance: **2.5 miles**
Elevation gain: **1,836 feet**
High point: **10,956 feet**
Rating: **Moderate**
Usually open: **June-September**
Topo: **USGS Mount of the Holy Cross, 1987**

The trail to spring-fed Whitney Lake begins on the Homestake Road, a historic route used by gold seekers. Today, the road provides access to some of the most breathtaking scenery in the Colorado Rockies. Dappled with lakes and cascading with waterfalls, the Homestake area is an unsurpassed natural resource for Eagle County. Water diversion plans threaten this beauty.

Drive to I-70 Dowd Junction exit 171 and turn south onto U.S. 24. Go 13 miles to the Homestake Road, no. 703. Turn right and drive 4.6 miles to the trailhead. Parking space is available on the road's left side. Bring insect repellent to ward off persistent flies on the lower trail.

The Homestake Road once served as an 1880s stagecoach route to the gold towns of Gold Park and Holy Cross City and a link to neighboring Missouri Camp and Camp Fancy. The stagecoaches brought travelers from the Denver & Rio Grande Railway station at bustling Red Cliff to these remote towns. Prospectors organized the Holy Cross Mining District in 1880. It expanded to an impressive 100 square miles during the 1880s boom years.

The trail climbs on an old closed road to a sagebrush hillside meadow thick with blossoms of the delicate mariposa lily in July. Beyond you'll enter a rich mature aspen forest with fire evidence.

A loose set of switchbacks appears as you approach 1 mile. While still in the trees you'll begin to hear the creek. At this point, look for an opening in the woods that offers a view southwest to the Homestake Dam. Also look for a nice view down to Whitney Creek where white water splashes against black boulders. Now, drop down to the creek and cross on a three-log bridge with a handrail. Climb out of the narrow creek canyon into a forest of pine and spruce. The trail winds through forest, then levels off as it approaches the lake. Note where you exited the woods near the lake to assure re-locating the trail.

Whitney Lake, at nearly 11,000 feet, pools beneath a rocky wall of 13,171-foot Whitney Peak. Encircled by spiky spruce, the tranquil lake reflects the ridge above and is constantly ringed with ripples made by rising fish. It thaws early, so June hikers may find the lake ice-free. Bring snacks for the gray jays, bold camp robbers who beg food from hikers.

J.D. Whitney escorted a group of Harvard Mining School graduates on a Colorado mine tour in 1869. He first named the Sawatch Range's Collegiate Peaks including Mount Harvard, 14,420 feet and Mount Yale, 14,196 feet.

Ski Touring/Snowshoeing (Easy): Although snowmobiles use the historic Homestake Road, the snowy route offers excellent snow tours because of its easy grade and freedom from avalanche danger, except near the dam.

Follow directions above to reach the Homestake Road and park in a wide spot near the turnoff. The trail begins at 8,920 feet and continues 11 miles to the Homestake Reservoir at 10,300 feet. Good shorter destinations along the snowy road route will satisfy snowshoers and skiers.

Homestake is a wide, glaciated valley gentle in terrain. A known elk winter range today, it once provided plentiful game and fish for 1800s settlers.

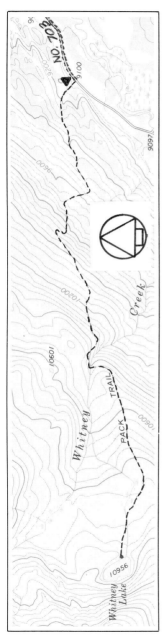

Snow-covered Homestake Road leads skiers to a long gentle valley perfect for touring. Only its terrain near Homestake Reservoir at 11 miles is avalanche-prone. Various destinations exist; the Whitney Lake trailhead at 4.6 miles makes a good turnaround. For hikers, Whitney Lake is a good June outing because the below-timberline lake thaws early. Bring snacks for hungry gray jays.

He makes me lie down in green pastures... He restores my soul. Ps. 23:2,3

Time: 5-6 hours
Distance: 3.9 miles
Elevation gain: 2,100 feet
High point: 11,400 feet
Rating: Moderate
Usually open: July-September
Topo: USGS Mount of the Holy Cross, 1987

The historic stagecoach route to Holy Cross City has in recent decades earned status as the most rough, challenging and bone-shattering four wheel drive road in the district. Corkscrew curves and yawning chasms below the road add zest. However, the road offers no problem to hikers except that it is steep. The route leaves 1880-founded Gold Park and climbs through aspen northwest to a meadow at 11,200 feet, then turns southwest for a short jog to the Holy Cross City ghost town. Echoes of an intriguing past whisper in the wind at the site of this 1880-built boom-bust gold town.

Drive 13 miles south on U.S. 24 from I-70 Dowd Junction exit 171 to the Homestake Road, no. 703. Turn right and proceed on good dirt road about 8 miles to the marked Holy Cross City jeep road. Park in the turn-around.

The trail travels over successive layers of rock ledge roadbed, then sections of old corduroy road. Where a side road enters from the left, keep right. Between 2.1 and 2.3 miles, the grade becomes moderate and, the terrain swampy. Resume climbing to the meadow at 2.9 miles where a signed fork directs you left for Holy Cross City. Another unsigned fork requires a second left. Walk uphill for 0.1 miles to a bench which offers views east to the Ten Mile Range. Skirt a major mudhole dug by mired jeeps in wet conditions. Continue to the remains of the Holy Cross stamp mill at 3.8 miles. Curve right to encounter a big grassy basin and the skeletons of several late 1800s structures.

Holy Cross boasted two ore mills. The one just below town on the road's west side was the big Holy Cross Mill, owned by the Gold Park Mining & Milling Company. A huge structure, the compartmentalized building stair-stepped down its sloping site, a jumble of multi-level roof shapes and angles. The mill connected to a sister mill below in Gold Park via a 2.5 mile flume running down the mountain. It processed ore from 28 claims. The Holy Cross Mill burned after a lightning strike many years ago. Identify the mill site by inspecting its flat top tailings pile. Mill tailings are finer than mine tailings.

Shafthouses and buildings are scattered across the mountainsides. Area mines included the Pelican, Molly, Comstock, Belle West, Tip Top, Backus and Hunkidori. The Pelican shaft house, a long, two-story rectangular structure, stood where a rubble rock pile lies alongside the roadway.

Ski Touring/Snowshoeing (Moderate): Although this ski tour travels a different route than the Holy Cross City trail, the two are connected by history. Ores from Holy Cross City rumbled in wagons down to Gold Park and then out on the Homestake Road to the Denver & Rio Grande rail line for transport to Denver. The "sister" ski tour is the Old Railroad Run, a 5.6 mile round-trip that uses the original 1881 narrow gauge railbed. The route passes two charcoal kilns used to make coke for railroad and ore smelter fuel.

Drive 19 miles from Minturn to the top of Tennessee Pass. On the right at the summit is the Tennessee Pass touring system trailhead. Five trail segments, each classified, signed and marked, combine to form a number of loops that offer easy to advanced challenge, powder to hardtrack. Ski right at the trailhead sign on a steady descent. Note the kilns at 0.6 miles. From their knoll location, views to the Minturn Cliffs, Sawatch peaks and Chicago Ridge appear. Pass the Powderhound Trail and drop to the Mitchell Creek valley at 2.8 miles. Return over the ski tracks on a moderate ascent.

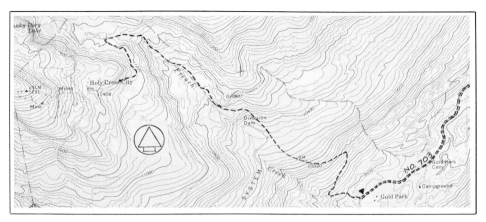

Seventeen foundations and a few ruined cabins mark the site of Holy Cross City, a timberline gold town that boomed and died by 1884. Main Street ran north-south through the meadow townsite. A school district, hotels including the Timberline, assay office, mine company headquarters and Frey's general store sprouted here.

At this signed fork the trail splits. Hikers go left for Holy Cross City; right for Hunky Dory and Seven Sisters Lakes.

Time: 5 hours
Distance: 4 miles
Elevation gain: 1,430 feet
High point: 11,550 feet
Rating: Moderate
Usually open: July-September
Topo: USGS Mount of the Holy Cross, 1987 and USGS Mount Jackson, 1987

A little paradise tucked away in an alpine basin, the 14 Missouri lakes and ponds provide an escape from everyday life to a place of sweet tranquility. Though a 1995 avalanche near the first lake buried the heavily-used trail, Forest Service workers have hacked out a hiker's path.

The trail begins above historic Gold Park. There a 400-strong population in 1881 enjoyed a postoffice with regular mail delivery by stage from Red Cliff, two hotels, a general store, notary, shoemaker and a 40-stamp mill which processed gold-bearing ore from area mines.

Drive 13 miles south on U.S. Highway 24 from I-70 Dowd Junction exit 171 to the Homestake Road, no. 703. Turn right and follow the Homestake Road past the Gold Park campground to County Road 704 at 8.5 miles. Turn right uphill on a rough road and drive west and southwest for 2.3 miles. Reach a T in the road at 10,200 feet and find the trailhead on the left. Park here.

The trail heads off left (southwest) along an overgrown road to the footpath at 0.5 miles. Turn right here and hike through woods. Cross Missouri Creek on a log bridge, then wind steeply upward near the rim of a deep crevasse. A wide bridge spans Missouri Creek here at about 1 mile. The view up and down the cascade-filled crevasse demands a stop. After another 0.2 miles of steep climb, emerge into a big, beautiful meadow where a moderate grade prevails from here to just before the lakes. Look for pink Parry's primrose and purple gentian (late August). Below the lakes, the trail parallels the creek. While water diversion dams and pipelines mar the trailhead area, the full volume of rushing Missouri Creek spills noisily through evergreens.

Ford a small stream and then a larger one before a sharp climb to the beautiful alpine basin that holds the Missouri Lakes. Soon a side trail left leads to the first of the lakes, a short climb of 100 feet gain in 0.3 miles. Savage Peak and its perpetual snowfield dominate the view to the south.

The main trail traverses the rocky, tree-dotted basin, a haven of lakes and flowers. This hike reaches its destination at the upper lake (4 miles, 11,550 feet altitude). For a falcon's view of the lake-dappled tundra bowl between Missouri and Fancy Passes, climb 11,986-foot Missouri Pass one-half mile beyond the upper lake. From the pass atop Holy Cross Ridge you can see Blodgett and Treasure Vault Lakes and the upper Cross Creek valley.

Float gold (gold eroded from veins in the rock) caused a rush here when the lone resident, a Frenchman, told prospectors of free gold that "lay thick at his cabin." By spring 1880, gold seekers had scrambled all over French Peak and Homestake Mountain, staking off claims. *The Summit County Times* in the nearby Ten Mile canyon town of Kokomo spread the news.

Missouri Camp, an 1880 mine settlement, sprang up at the confluence of Missouri and Fancy Creeks. Instead of the usual haphazard jumble of cabins and tents, town founders planned their community, laying out streets parallel to the creek. Today, trees obscure the camp's neat foundations.

Miners here transported ores to the Gold Park Mining & Milling

Company's 40-stamp processing mill below in Gold Park. This 1880-founded company town still had a two-story community house and eight cabins dotted across its meadow location in 1942 when the U.S. Army used the area for an artillery range. Later in 1970, two cabins remained, along with an 1880s cemetery below the present campground. Cairns mark miners' graves.

In winter, 1881, a blacksmith laid off by the company during snowbound months became enraged and murdered H. Weston, the mine company foreman. The malcontent also attempted to kill the superintendent. The irate blacksmith, named Bagley, then fortified himself in his cabin. Townsmen besieged the log structure for eight hours before hitting on a plan. They "covered" a volunteer who broke for the cabin and laid down an ample amount of mine blasting powder. After the cabin blew up, they found Bagley's body with a bullet hole in his heart.

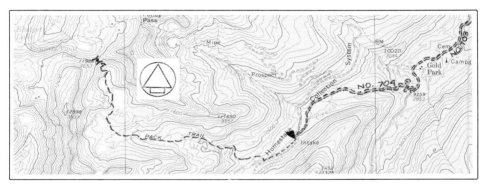

One of 14 Missouri Lakes pools in a green basin below Missouri Pass. Climb to its summit for falcon's view of the lake dappled bowl between this pass and Fancy. From the summit, which straddles Holy Cross Ridge, hikers will view Blodgett and Treasure Vault Lakes and the upper Cross Creek valley.

And Fall Creek Pass

Time: 6-8 hours
Distance: 5 miles
Elevation gain: 2,300 feet
High point: 12,580 feet
Rating: More difficult
Usually open: July-September
Topo: USGS Mount of the Holy Cross, 1987

Seven lovely sisters surrounded by breathtaking mountain scenery await hikers enroute to Fall Creek Pass. On the pass' 12,580-foot summit, you straddle magnificent Holy Cross Ridge with views east to the massive Ten Mile Range. This trail's beauty has no equal.

Drive 13 miles south of I-70 Dowd Junction exit 171 on U.S. 24 to the Homestake Road, no. 703. Turn right and proceed along good gravel road past the Gold Park Campground to a side road at 8.5 miles, County Road 704. Turn right onto this rough road and drive west/southwest for 2.3 miles. Reach a T at 10,200 feet and turn right. Go north 2 miles, passing a junction at about 1 mile where you keep right and go slightly downhill (avoiding the uphill left switchback). Park in a level area beside a jeep road that leads straight ahead. The main road continues uphill left to a diversion dam.

The 4WD road straight ahead connects within 50 yards to the Holy Cross City jeep road. Your drive has eliminated an uphill trek on that road to reach this point. If you hesitate to drive the rough route to this trailhead, walk up the Holy Cross City 4WD road from Gold Park (see directions for hike no. 28).

The trail begins on a short section of 4WD road that quickly intersects with the Holy Cross City road. Turn left onto this historic route. Climb alongside French Creek for about 1.5 miles to a large meadow at 11,200 feet where the road forks just beyond a creek crossing. The road to the left goes to Holy Cross City, a historic 1880s gold camp now a ghost town, a 1-2 hour side trip. (no. 28.)

The right fork leads to Hunky Dory Lake and Seven Sisters Lakes. The trail circles the east side of the large meadow and then climbs into the Holy Cross Wilderness to Hunky Dory Lake. Named for a nearby gold mine, it is the first of many splendid tarns along the trail to Fall Creek Pass. Just past it lie the remains of a cabin and some rusted mine machinery. A waterfall on French Creek may also catch your eye. The trail follows French Creek, climbing moderately here, then rises sharply to rock-punctuated meadows above timberline. Mt. Whitney, 13,271 feet, comes into view at right.

The Seven Sisters Lakes start with the smallest and gain in size as you approach Fall Creek Pass. The trail levels off among the lakes, allowing hikers to catch their breath for the 1.5 mile tramp up the pass.

Catching one's breath is difficult because the scenery is breathtaking. The seven shining sisters hide among wildflower-upholstered knolls and benches, then surprise hikers with their individual beauty. Look for rosy queens crown; listen for marmot, or whistle pig.

Ski Touring/Snowshoeing (More difficult): 1800s gold miners got around in winter on skis—the kind that weighed 15 pounds and measured four inches wide and 12 feet long. They skied all over this region. While this tour does not travel to the lakes, it does enter a nearby valley frequented by miners.

Drive past the Homestake Road south 1.4 miles to No Name Road, no. 705.

A number of trails penetrate the gulch and the map below details their routes. This trail, No Name Loop, is a one hour, 1.6 miles round-trip. Travel the snow-covered No Name Road to a spot where the road hairpins left at 0.7 miles, then after 300 yards turns again on a sharp right. As soon as the road straightens out, look for a directional arrow pointing left. Cross No Name Gulch to begin a quick drop down the valley. Enjoy snow that stays soft and powdery through the mid-winter months. Bend left at a meadow near 1.3 miles to connect again with the No Name Road.

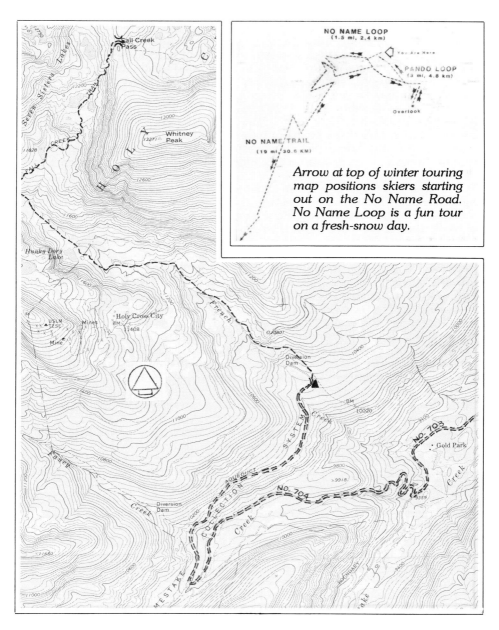

Arrow at top of winter touring map positions skiers starting out on the No Name Road. No Name Loop is a fun tour on a fresh-snow day.

31   FANCY LAKE

Time: 4 hours
Distance: 3.0 miles
Elevation gain: 1,260 feet
High point: 11,540 feet
Rating: More difficult
Usually open: July-September
Topo: USGS Mount of the Holy Cross, 1987

Joe Fancy's bustling mine camp sprang up in the early 1880s with 20 cabins and a water-powered stamp mill to process local ores. The camp's boom paralleled that of the entire mine-pocketed area above Homestake Creek. But by 1883, the frenzy fizzled and Camp Fancy, along with the others, saw its population dwindle.

Drive 13 miles south on U.S. 24 from I-70 Dowd Junction exit 171 to the Homestake Road, no. 703. Turn right and proceed past the Gold Park Campground to mile 8.5. Turn right here onto County Road 704, a rough dirt road leading to the Missouri Lakes and Fancy Lake trailheads. Drive uphill generally west and southwest for 2.3 miles to a T at 10,200 feet. The trailhead is at left.

The trail has been rerouted to avoid a diversion dam, part of Aurora and Colorado Springs' massive Homestake water diversion project. The new trail quickly enters the undisturbed Holy Cross Wilderness. It switchbacks up to the creek and crosses Fancy Creek on a new bridge just past 1 mile above the trailhead. An old mining road, recently improved for better drainage, follows the northeast bank of Fancy Creek. Later, the route becomes a footpath. Continue upward, then travel near the rim of a deep rocky ravine. After a meadow marked with cairns, ford another larger stream, then cross the clearing to its upper end where the foot trail becomes more distinct.

During the last 0.3 miles, the trail may fade. The path climbs through trees for a few hundred feet to a more open area. Here keep left for the trail. Then scale a grassy rock-strewn hillside for several hundred feet. The trail fades out here but you are close to the lake. Curve right and ascend in open terrain on a northwesterly course. (Use a compass and map if necessary.) The last brief section is a steep climb to the southeast shore of Fancy Lake.

The lake lies in a stark setting near timberline. The gray rock walls beyond sweep down from Holy Cross Ridge in a raw, craggy cirque. Above and north, a steep road makes the dizzying climb to Fancy Pass.

Ski Touring/Snowshoeing (Easy): The No Name Road, a neighbor to the Homestake-Fancy Creek area, offers a serene ski tour.

Drive 1.4 miles south of the Homestake Road on U.S. 24 to the No Name Road, no. 705, and park on the right. The unplowed road rises to a series of switchbacks then heads southwest into quiet conifer forest.

Below is the site of early-day Pando and Camp Hale. The name Pando probably came from the Spanish word meaning "slow water." The settlement sprang up with development of the railroad, after its mine camp neighbors, Eagle City and Mitchell Cabins. A man named Roudebush built the first cabin at Eagle Park's upper end (today's Camp Hale site) after Frank Benjamin and C. C. Welch discovered placer gold just south of present-day Pando. The Denver & Rio Grande, linking silver boom towns of Leadville and Red Cliff, laid track here in 1881. Ice ponds, still visible in the area, provided ice for railroad refrigeration needs. Later, when Camp Hale came in 1942, a D&RG

railway tunnel was built on the rocky hillside above Pando to relocate track from Camp Hale's valley floor location. The U.S. Army camp, set across the valley on the Eagle River's east side, trained Tenth Mountain Division skiing soldiers for World War II combat duty in the severe weather and mountain terrain of Alaska and northern Italy's Alps.

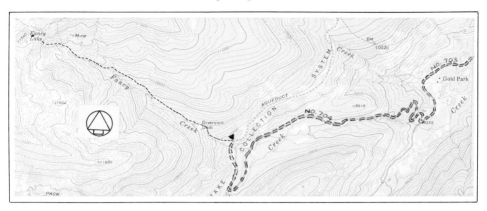

Fancy Lake has its shores "sugared" with snow on a September morning. The old Fancy Pass mining road offers several side trips: Go right on the Fancy road for Mulhall Lakes, Holy Cross City or Cleveland Lake. (The trip to Mulhall requires a climb from the trail fork where you go left.)

Time: 8 hours
Distance: 10 miles (loop)
Elevation gain: 2,550 feet
High point: 12,380 feet
Rating: Most difficult
Usually open: Mid-July-September
Topo: USGS Mount of the Holy Cross and USGS Mount Jackson, 1987

How huge timbers and heavy iron ore processing machinery for Treasure Vault mill construction ever came over 12,380-foot Fancy Pass remains an intriguing question. The raw, rubble-rock pass over craggy Holy Cross Ridge, once knife-sharp at top, now offers a narrow passage courtesy of miners with dynamite. The pass overlooks an isolated alpine bowl that cradles Treasure Vault and Blodgett Lakes. Visible beyond is 11,986-foot Missouri Pass. Hikers cross it, then drop down to the flower-filled basin holding the Missouri Lakes, an unforgettable tour in mid-summer.

Drive to the trailhead, using directions for Missouri Lakes Trail, no. 29.

The trail: Walk 0.3 miles north from the trailhead parking area past Fancy Creek to the Fancy Lake-Fancy Pass 4WD road at left. Follow a trail that switchbacks uphill to cross Fancy Creek at 1 mile and reach Fancy Lake, 11,540 feet at 3 miles. Use directions for hike no. 31, Fancy Lake, especially for guidance where the footpath fades. The alpine lake makes a good rest stop.

To find the pass route, circle right to the lake's north side. Cross the creek flowing from Fancy Lake, walking east and north. Make a short, sharp scramble up the gully north of the lake to arrive at the very steep rock-paved Fancy Pass Road. This mining road comes up from Holy Cross City (hike no. 28) to mount challenging Fancy Pass. Turn left and climb the short (0.5 miles) but taxing ascent to the pass summit. Keep a sharp eye for the faint trail on switchbacks close to the top.

Now we will answer our own question: How did mine equipment make it over this pass? The Treasure Vault Mill's mine timbers, boilers and huge iron stamps were dragged cross-country up to Fancy's summit, then lowered over the sheer cliffs on the west side by hand, without use of the pass road. Steel pins, driven into rock walls, supported cable and pulleys to carry the load. Once the load was down, hard-working mules, which had hauled the heavy-laden wagons up the pass, now dragged the load to the Cross Creek valley's head. All this physical effort thwarted an order from the Fancy Pass road owners, the Gold Park Mining & Milling Company. They had denied road use to the competitive Treasure Vault Mine. A skeleton of the mill remained till 1959 and now lies in shambles.

This pass, named for 1880s prospector Joe Fancy, commands views east to the Ten Mile Range from Peak One past the dramatic Mayflower and Clinton amphitheaters. Pacific Peak juts up and beyond rises Quandary, a fourteener. Farther south stretches the Mosquito Range. West are the lakes, Missouri Pass and the head of the long Cross Creek valley leading to Minturn.

While geometric-shape rocks and frequent high winds hazard the pass' eastern approach, a somewhat better trail lies on the west side. Watch out when it's snowy—the trail becomes very slippery.

Soon the path intersects the Cross Creek Trail (no. 20) where you continue left to a wet flower basin cut by tiny streams. Pass Treasure Vault Lake. Blodgett is the big lake to the west. Then make the short climb to Missouri Pass. Massive Savage Peak to the south protects the lake-dotted bowl. The plunging view to the Missouri Lakes is worth a rest stop on the rocky benches.

Descend to a trail that winds among the idyllic Missouri Lakes, cross the 1995 avalanche debris, then follow Missouri Creek down to two scenic crossings on bridges in the creek ravine. Finally, the trail passes another dam and then forks left (avoid the dusty right fork) near the aqueduct road to end.

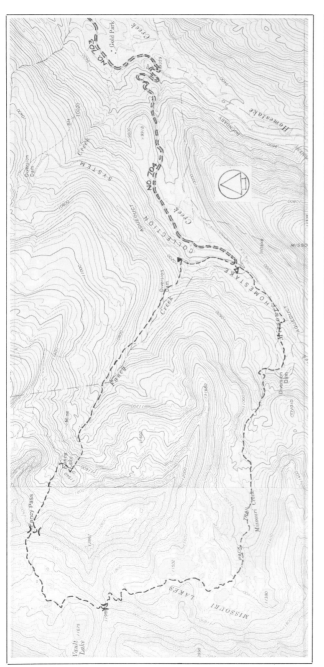

High in the Holy Cross Wilderness lies an alpine world of raw rock and fragile flowers. This lake-studded hideaway gives hikers a unique experience with the scenic natural re-source Eagle County is working to shelter and preserve. Rocky benches just below the Missouri Pass sign invite hikers to stop and enjoy a plung-ing view to Missouri Lakes below.

33   LONESOME LAKE

Time: 5-6 hours
Distance: 5.2 miles
Elevation gain: 1,560 feet
High point 11,560 feet
Rating: Moderate
Usually open: July-September
Topo: USGS Homestake Reservoir, 1970

Getting to an isolated, flower-rimmed glacial lake in the primitive Holy Cross Wilderness usually requires perspiration! But not Lonesome Lake. Clear and blue-green below a soaring 12,200-foot ridge that divides Eagle and Lake counties, the lake makes a satisfying spot to rest, take pictures, explore.

Drive 13 miles south of I-70 Dowd Junction exit 171 on U.S. 24 to the Homestake Road, no. 703. Proceed 10.5 miles on this well-maintained gravel road to a signed junction below the Homestake Reservoir where a road intersects from left. Park.

The trail, re-routed in the 1990s, now skirts water diversion pipe. This segment provides the only real climb on the route, which quickly connects to the old footpath.

Walk on a pleasant grade through woods to the north edge of the first of two long meadows. Elephant head, with its clustered fuschia flower, grows here. Some old cabins remain across the meadow, left. The trail, smooth and level, invites you to stretch your legs. After one level mile, emerge from the meadow to climb in forest. Cross a small stream and enter the second meadow. Here you walk just above the open area in scattered trees. Near the meadow's end, hikers must pick a route through avalanche debris. The steep chutes above look quite capable of causing this damage. If the trail fades in any of several areas ahead, keep left. Walk the top of a small grassy ridge, then, for the next mile, wind upward through the woods.

Step into a big lush, basin contoured by green knolls and benches. Note where you emerged from the woods for the return. The trail plays hide and seek in this mountain-walled glacial valley. If you lose the trail, travel generally southeast (left). Because the valley narrows as you climb, you have no chance of missing the lake nestled above in the final cirque. Find the flower-dotted grassy hill in the middle of the high valley. Hike up this rise and see the lake beyond some gray slag rock and little ponds, sometimes dry in late summer.

Lonesome Lake curves like a comma, with East Homestake Creek flowing from its northwest tip. Beyond the ridge that towers south of the tarn, it's just two miles as the crow flies to Lake County's Turquoise Lake.

Cutthroat trout as large as 14 inches are reputed to live in Lonesome Lake. If you miss out on the fish, watch for elk and deer on the return trip.

Ski Touring/Snowshoeing (More difficult): A 5-mile plus loop atop Tennessee Pass straddles the county line and Continental Divide not far from Lonesome Lake. Drive 23 miles south of Minturn to the pass summit and turn right into the trailhead parking area. Signed trails with trailhead maps provide a variety of winter trails from a short 2.5 mile powder-lovers route to the 7.3 mile steep-drop Mitchell Creek Loop.

Begin on the Railroad Run and follow signs for Powderhound to the CD Junction. Then travel south to the Colorado Trail. Follow the Colorado Trail back to the parking area. Trails Illustrated, Tennessee Pass, maps these routes.

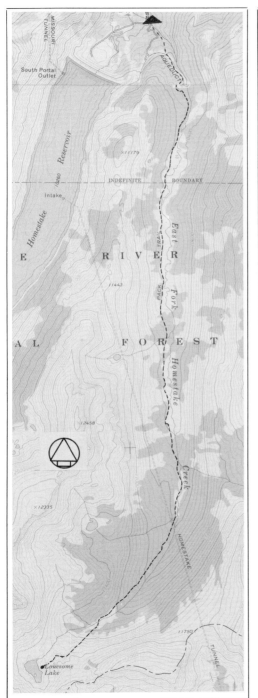

An easy walk in the Holy Cross Wilderness takes hikers to Lonesome Lake, a little-used but delightful destination in the Homestake Reservoir area.

Kids' Hike to Cataract Falls:

Time: 5-6 hours
Distance: 4 miles
Elevation gain: 2,422 feet
High point: 12,200 feet
Rating: More difficult
Usually open: July to September
Topo: USGS Pando and USGS Copper Mountain, 1987

Time: 2 hours
Distance: 0.7 miles
Elevation gain: 200 feet
High point: 9,640 feet
Rating: Easy

Camp Hale, the nation's highest U.S. Army base, burst into being in 1941 when the war in Europe required an elite corps of skiing soldiers. The U.S. Army's Tenth Mountain Division, headquartered at Camp Hale, scrambled on skis and C-rations all over Kokomo Pass, the Ten Mile Canyon, Cooper Hill, Tennessee Pass and the Homestake valley, learning to endure every extreme that mountain terrain and weather could deal out. Baptized by German gunfire in the Italian Alps, the fighting Tenth took vital Mt. Belvedere, Riva Ridge and the Po Valley, a key contribution to the Allied victory.

Drive U.S. 24, also named the Tenth Mountain Division Memorial Highway, 15.4 miles from I-70 Dowd Junction exit 171. You will pass the Homestake Road at 13 miles. Look for a railroad bridge at about 15.2 miles. Just past that bridge is the north entrance to Camp Hale. Turn left here. At the first fork, go right. Proceed 1.1 mile. Come to a fork with the Resolution Creek Road, no. 702. Go south here 0.5 miles to another fork. You'll be on the Eagle River Road, no. 714. Drive from the fork to the fenced trailhead parking, 3.9 miles total. (For the Kids' Hike, shorten this segment, parking at 3.2 miles.)

The Kids' Hike trail to Cataract Falls is located near the road fork by a "Restricted Bridge" sign. The signed Colorado Trail lies just left of the road. It parallels the road, rising and falling for 0.7 miles to a wood bridge and waterfall.

The trail to Kokomo Pass begins on a two-wheel track which ends at a waterfall in a steep gorge on Cataract Creek. Turn right here. The first section labors up an old wagon road through thick aspen groves that turn solid gold in September. Drop to cross Cataract Creek and climb in rich aspen forest. After 1 mile, the wagon road ends in a meadow that holds remains of old buildings, a crumbled bridge and signs of a cabin fire on the creek's right side.

Continue east on the left side of Cataract Creek to a steep slope which alternates deep forest and small meadows. Climb some tight switchbacks, then break out from the trees to a big alpine bowl. The well-marked path rises southeast (right) through the large basin. Trail builders originally created excellent signage and carefully-built cairns to direct hikers. The cairns were destroyed. Soon the green saddle that is Kokomo Pass appears. Colorado Trail construction volunteers once marked the summit with a huge cairn, now gone, which sheltered September hikers caught in a flash snowstorm.

Views east sweep across the upper Ten Mile valley to Fremont Pass and the now-closed Climax Molybdenum Mine. Several tailings lakes testify to the millions of ore tons of "gray gold" mined since the 1920s. Robinson, a Victorian town which once flourished in McNulty Gulch, is submerged in tailings muck. Look west for views of the Sawatch Range. Kokomo Pass, traveled by Kokomo town miners enroute to Red Cliff, straddles a mountain range rich in silver.

Ski Touring/Snowshoeing (Most difficult): Camp Hale offers a variety of delightful tours, some easy, some challenging. This tour, which offers skiers a roller-coaster ride down the Tenth Mountain Division's B slope, is challenging. But you can skip this hill, returning on your original tracks.

The Camp Hale Loop, a 5-mile tour along the Eagle River and then onto its East Fork, starts at the south entrance to Camp Hale. Drive U.S. 24 17.5 miles from I-70 Dowd Junction exit 171 to the south gate. This gate is 0.8 miles past the aging remains of the wartime main gate at left. Park in the plowed turnout.

Begin past the snow-covered fishing pond just off the highway, then turn right and gradually curve left to meet the Eagle's East Fork. Cross the river and glide into the trees on a roadcut, which is not shown on the map. At mile 3 the trail intersects the old U.S. 24 roadbed. Turn around and go west on it. At mile 4, the advanced skier can climb the B slope for an exciting downhill north-northwest on open hillside. Then rejoin original trail back to the pondside parking area. Be aware of Nova Guide's use of the valley for snowmobiling.

Snowshoers, try the Kids' Trail to the waterfall (see directions above) then continue on the Colorado Trail as it climbs toward Tennessee Pass.

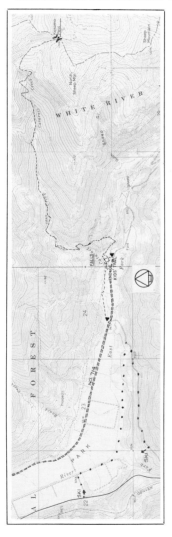

Kokomo Pass straddles a mountain range rich in silver. Robinson (above), once bigger than booming Red Cliff, lay below the pass. Its miners and those from Kokomo used the pass to travel to Red Cliff.

A panorama of Fremont Pass peaks is seen from Kokomo Pass during a break in a September snowstorm. Views west are to the Sawatch Range.

Time: 3 hours
Distance: 6.5 miles
Elevation loss: 1,048 feet
High point: 10,424 feet
Rating: Easy
Usually open: Late June-September
Topo: USGS Leadville North and Pando

With ice-encrusted army-issue socks frozen to his boots, a skiing soldier from the U.S. Army Tenth Mountain Division forced numb fingers to work his boot laces. He had gone to bed in snow after dark and now struggled in pre-dawn darkness to awake for ski training on Tennessee Pass. The year was 1944. The soldier was stationed at Camp Hale, the destination of this downhill walk.

Hikers can exercise their imaginations as well as their quads on a history-rich route from the 10,424-foot Tennessee summit to the ruins of Camp Hale.

Two cars are required for this one-way hike. Take one car to the Camp Hale trailhead using directions for trail no. 34.

Drive a second car south on U.S. 24 to the Tennessee Pass summit. Turn right into the parking area. Col. John C. Fremont discovered this pass in summer, 1845 enroute to California. William Henry Jackson, in his quest to photograph the elusive Mount of the Holy Cross, crossed the pass in August, 1873 with his darkroom-toting mule, Hypo.

The trail begins at the signed trailhead and advances west into dry conifer forest. Coke ovens remain nearby from Leadville's mining days. From 1887 to 1895, workers slowly fired green pine in these beehive-shaped rock kilns to create charcoal. Freighters hauled the charcoal to Leadville, where ore smelters used it as fuel. The narrow gauge railways also consumed charcoal to fire their locomotives. The historic Denver & Rio Grande built its roadbed here in 1881.

Watch for a fork to take you right downhill. Next, the Colorado Trail, well-marked with trail signs, crosses a logged area punctuated by two-foot high stumps. (Loggers in the high country cut the trees at snow level during winter; sometimes stumps are six feet high. Later they skidded the cut logs out over the snow, an easy method of transport.)

After traversing a pleasant pine forest with a grassy floor, views to the Collegiate Range command hikers' attention. Then a marshy wetlands provides both sudden contrast and big vistas. Cross the Eagle River on a sawn-log bridge, then pass railroad remains and a gate before crossing Highway 24 at 10,000 feet altitude. Pick up the signed Colorado Trail again.

Walk north 1.8 miles to cross a forest road. Along the way, stop to enjoy the bench on a view promontory. The trail dips and rises through cool, thick pine forest with several openings, including one at the stream crossing. Pick up the roadway for 1.1 mile. Next you will traverse the Tenth Mountain Division's ski training hill, the B slope, which the lodgepole forest is slowly reclaiming. Enjoy the big view of Camp Hale from the opening here. Imagine rows of buildings on neatly arranged streets there—enough buildings to house 17,000. Finally, descend on switchbacks to Camp Hale near the old shooting range.

Skiing soldier Scollay Parker remembers the hefty size and weight of his D-Series pack on a Tennessee Pass march. "Mine was so heavy that to get it on my shoulders I had to lie down on the ground, put my shoulders through the straps, roll over on my hands and knees, and finally stand up in a forward-leaning position." In contrast, he winces "...they instructed us never to load on a mule more than one-third of his weight!"

Ski touring/Snowshoeing (Moderate): A 3-mile ski or snowshoe tour to a wide meadow above Vance's Cabin makes a great 3-4 hour outing. Park in the Ski Cooper lot at left on the pass summit. (Ski Cooper originated as the Tenth's main downhill ski trail, and once boasted the world's longest T-bar, 6,100 feet.) Ski left of the lodge building to get the trail.

Follow the aqueduct road 0.6 miles, cross Piney Creek, then turn onto a trail at left. Blue diamonds mark the route through a beautiful old-growth spruce-fir forest. Then the trail veers left from the creek drainage to climb a 500-foot slope. This tough, but short, open hillside demands climbing skills. The trail later rolls and turns in deep forest, then emerges from the trees to a meadow studded with snags from an old burn. The mottled amber wood trunks look like sculpture. Study their patterns. We saw a Picasso drawing.

The 11,000-foot meadow, with its breathless descent, is your destination. Try slalom turns among the snags or ski a pleasant loop around the meadow.

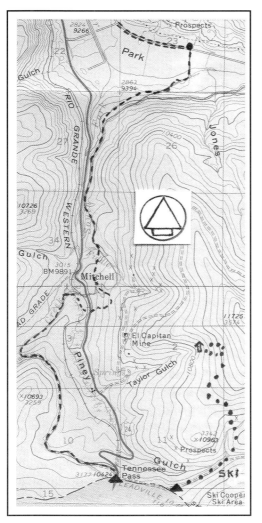

This segment of the 480-mile Colorado Trail resonates with history. Charles Wheaton built a road over Tennessee Pass in September, 1879, launching a stagecoach line for passengers and supplies. A few years later, the Denver & Rio Grande railway scaled the pass to serve area camps and mines near Gilman and Red Cliff.

Trails near Piney Lake

36   PINEY RIVER FALLS

Time: 3-4 hours
Distance: 2.8 miles
Elevation gain: 560 feet
High point: 9,920 feet
Rating: Moderate
Usually open: June-September
Topo: USGS Eagle County, 1975, Sheet 2

A crystal cascade on the roiling Piney River makes a cool destination for a hike from the scenic Piney Lake area. Much photographed for the grandeur of its alpine setting and much-publicized for its abundant water (which the Denver Water Board wants), Piney Lake and the Eagles Nest Wilderness beyond offer hikers majestic natural beauty.

Drive 1 mile west from Vail Village I-70 exit 176 on the North Frontage Road to Red Sandstone Road. Turn right. Drive 0.7 miles to a fork and go left onto County Road no. 700, a good gravel road leading to Piney Lake. Drive a total of 11 miles to the entrance to Piney Lake and Piney River Ranch. Turn right and park outside the first wooden gate, off ranch property.

The trail begins from the parking lot's north side. You walk above Piney Lake's north shore on a trail recently re-routed to the northern slope above the lake. At a fork the Soda Lakes/Meadow Creek Trail will go left and this trail, the Piney River Trail, continues right.

Enter the Eagles Nest Wilderness area immediately. The footpath travels above a broad flat valley beyond Piney Lake. When the trail begins to climb in the aspen-pine forest, fallen trees, roots and rocks will obstruct progress.

The path ascends up and around the rocky cirque that makes the Piney Lake valley so photogenic. Where the trail forks at several points, keep right. Up on the ridge, cross several small streams, then arrive at a rock-walled scenic overlook. This natural viewing stand offers a long view down the pastoral valley to Piney Lake. Less than 10 minutes beyond this spot is the waterfall, this hike's destination. The falls visit involves a few moments of scrambling but the seclusion and wild beauty provide a reward. The falls, a fizzy whitewater cascade, pours over black boulders with an occasional icy spray on bystanders.

Hikers wishing to continue beyond the falls will encounter beautiful scenery on a trail tricky to follow. The continuing Piney River Trail offers backpackers a route to Upper Piney Lake at 9 miles and access for advanced hikers to 13,534-foot Mt. Powell. Serious mountaineers can also scale West Booth Pass, 11,980 feet, to gain access to the Booth Creek drainage.

Lower Red Sandstone Creek played a role in Vail's history. Frank and Marge Haas bought 520 acres on the creek around 1938. The ranchland later came into the hands of John Hanson, who sold it to John Conway, a Vail Mountain developer. In need of base area land and reluctant to announce this to the world, Conway, along with Peter Seibert, Earl Eaton and Bob Fowler, formed the Transmontane Rod and Gun Club, a group interested in property "for sporting use." Purchasing the Hanson land for $110 an acre, they made it the site of Vail village. The nearby Katsos Ranch, purchased for $75,000, gave the village another 500 acres. The Vail ski mountain opened in 1962.

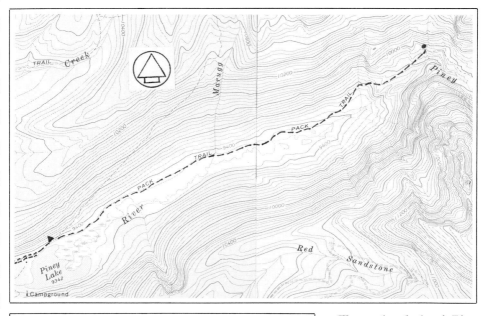

The cool splash of Piney River Falls awaits hikers who begin the trail at scenic Piney Lake above the town of Vail. Flowers proliferate along the path. Look for columbine in late June and early July, monkshood, harebell and mariposa lily.

Then shall all the trees of the wood sing for joy; for he comes to judge the earth. Ps. 96:12,13

91

Time: 3-4 hours
Distance: 3 miles
Elevation gain: 1,480 feet
High point: 10,880 feet
Rating: More difficult
Usually open: June-September
Topo: USGS Eagle County, 1975, Sheet 2

If you want a workout on a short hike from a superb setting, try this 3-mile trek to Marugg Creek on the Soda Lakes Trail. Starting at beautiful Piney Lake is a bonus. The hike will introduce backpackers to the Soda Lake route's possibilities: A climb to Elliott Ridge for a walk along the skyscraping spine of the Gore Range and a longer loop trip to Pretty Mountain.

Drive 1 mile west from Vail Village I-70 exit 176 on the North Frontage Road to Red Sandstone Road. Turn right. Drive 0.7 miles to a fork and continue left on County Road 700, a good gravel road leading to Piney Lake. Drive 11 miles total to the Piney River Ranch-Piney Lake entrance. Turn right and park off ranch property outside the first wooden gate at 11 miles.

The trail begins from the parking lot's north side. You walk above Piney Lake's north shore on a trail recently re-routed to the northern slope above the lake. At a fork choose the Soda Lakes/Meadow Creek trail at left, which is the route to Marugg Creek. The Piney River Trail on the right goes to Piney River Falls (hike no. 36) and on to Upper Piney Lake.

Mount a demanding slope among rich aspen with views to Piney Lake and its pastoral valley. Above the big, flat basin northeast rises the rugged Gore Range. The trail switchbacks, levels off, then climbs again. The quaking aspen forest turns to spruce and fir. Cross a small fork of Marugg Creek, then follow the creek up to ford the main flow. (This route does not appear on the USGS map.) A wooden sign marks the crossing as Marugg Creek. This quiet streamside spot makes a good lunch stop and destination.

The Soda Lakes Trail continues, providing plenty of choices for advanced hikers. Connecting trails offer a loop trip just above. The trail passes the intersection with the East Meadow Creek Trail and climbs east of Pretty Mountain to a junction at 11,247 feet. (See the USGS Piney Peak topo for this.) Make a sharp left at this junction and head downhill south on a jog that soon meets the East Meadow Creek Trail. Later, follow the base of 11,268-foot Pretty Mountain and curve around to the east. Intersect the main Meadow Creek Trail and cross Meadow Creek heading uphill northeast to rejoin the original Soda Creek Trail where you began the loop.

Advanced hikers can climb to Elliott Ridge at nearly 12,000 feet. To reach the ridge requires a 6-mile climb that gains about 2,600 total feet of altitude. Use the Piney Peak topo for the trail connection at 11,955 feet.

Ranchers along Red Sandstone and Meadow Creeks often faced problems caused by the area's abundant wildlife. An early sheep rancher, tired of losing lambs to a mountain lion, built a brush corral. To bait the predator, he herded the lambs into the corral and climbed a pine tree above to await his prey. He settled on a branch, readied his rifle and waited. He became bored and began studying the branches above. There crouched the mountain lion, eyes fixed on the lambs. The startled rancher fell from the tree, breaking his shoulder. Finally, a forest ranger found him and hauled him off to a doctor in Minturn.

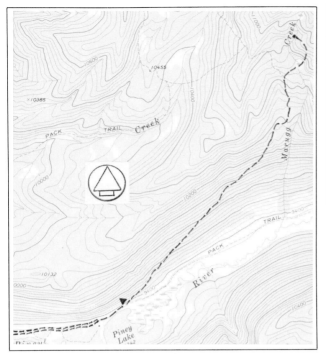

The topo map does not show this trail's junction with Marugg Creek. But the path does meet the creek in a cool crossing area which becomes this hike's destination.

Teenage hiker enjoys Piney Lake's placid beauty. The Marugg Creek hike enters the Gore Range Wilderness at the trailhead and climbs an aspen slope with Piney Lake views. Visitors will enjoy the drive to the Piney trailhead. Deer hide in the trees while flocks of sheep often cover open slopes. Views of the Vail Ski Mountain appear on the return.

Time: **3 hours**
Distance: **3.75 miles**
Elevation gain: **531 feet**
High point: **10,158 feet**
Rating: **Easy**
Usually open: **June-September**
Topo: **USGS Vail West, 1987**

Bring grapes to feed the hungry gray jays at Lost Lake. The camp robbers are tame enough to pose for pictures and bold enough to eat from your hand. Bring the kids, too. Spring-fed, fresh and fun to cool your toes in, Lost Lake makes a good goal for hikers of all ages, school-age to seniors.

Drive west 1 mile from Vail village I-70 exit 176 on the North Frontage Road. At Red Sandstone Road, turn right. Drive 0.7 miles to a fork and continue left on County Road 700, a good gravel road all the way to the trailhead. At 3.3 miles note a road to Lost Lake; this is the motorized route. Stay on the main road to mile 7.2. Trailhead parking area is on the right.

The trail follows a ridge that separates the Piney and Red Sandstone drainages. Thick lodgepole pine covers the north-dropping Piney slope while aspen grows on the trail's south side, the Red Sandstone drainage. A nearly level footpath leads hikers straight northeast, then turns right for a quick drop to Lost Lake.

The path begins with a fork, the first of three. For the first fork go either way. The two trails join. At the second fork, an old trail heads downhill left to the Piney drainage. Go straight. The third fork branches off down a steep slope on a 1-mile route to Piney Lake. Continue straight ahead. Trail signs give confusing numbers. The Lost Lake Trail's official number is 1893.

The trail dips and rolls but remains generally level. Occasional breaks in the tree cover allow views to Vail Mountain (south) and the mountains along Piney Ridge—Piney Peak, 11,559 feet and Cottonwood, 11,440 feet.

Lost Lake, a peaceful, spring-fed, pine-rimmed mountain lake, receives use from 4WD enthusiasts as well as campers. Human impact here could spoil a beautiful natural resource. The Forest Service requests that campers use a stove for cooking, camp 200 feet from the shore and pack out all trash.

Ski Touring/Snowshoeing (Most difficult): The winter route uses the snow-covered road to the Lost Lake motorized vehicle access road and then a cruise along on timber road to the lake. For this route, use the hiker's driving directions to the fork at 0.7 miles on Red Sandstone Road. Then climb 2.6 miles to an intersection signed for Lost Lake motorized trails (right). After this fork, three more intersections will confront you. Go left at each junction. Less than 0.3 miles after the third intersection, come to a sharp right-hand turn in the road at 10,063 feet. A meadow lies just ahead (north). Here strike off northwest for a 0.9 miles climb to the lake.

This trail, 12.6 miles round trip, earns a most difficult rating because of the demands of the 6.3 mile uphill stretch.

A snowmobile outfitter uses the Red Sandstone Road. Machines groom the surface—nice for ski skaters. The operator promises that guides will slow down for cross-country skiers and snowshoers. Individuals also snowmobile here but their use is low.

Along with the Lost Lake Road at 2.6 miles, winter recreationists can tour the Red and White Mountain Road.

Sheep ranchers exploring the backcountry on horseback tramped out trails in the Lost Lake and Piney region. Many of Eagle County's trails formed from centuries of use by migrating buffalo and nomadic Ute Indians.

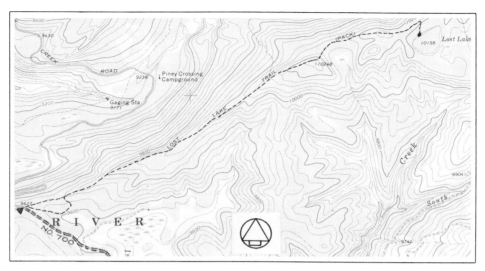

Picnickers won't find ants at Lost Lake but they will encounter the grey Canadian Jay. His hearty appetite and lack of timidity make him a persistent lunchtime guest. You'll soon have him eating out of your hand.

Time: 2-4 hours
Distance: 2.4 miles
Elevation gain: 1,500 to overlook; 2,140 feet to lake
High point: 12,000 feet
Rating: Most difficult
Usually open: July-September
Topo: USGS Vail East

We approached Crater Lake in a gauzy mist. Icy gray veiled the green plunge to the 11,320-foot lake from the rickracked edge of the big bowl encasing it. Awed by its beauty in the August snow shower, we vowed to revisit this cradled tarn on a blue-sky day.

It's a long haul by 4-wheel drive to reach the Eiseman Hut area where the indistinct trail begins—but worth the effort.

Speaking of effort, this trail is rated "Most difficult" not for its demand for stamina (though it demands some) but for its sketchy trail. Route-finding skills are necessary at this writing. More use will eventually create a defined trail. Wear a sturdy boot with a good tread for this trail's rocky section and if you use hiking poles, bring them along.

Drive 1 mile west from the main Vail Village roundabout along the North Frontage Road to Red Sandstone Road. Turn right. Drive 0.7 miles to a fork, and go left onto the Piney Lake Road, no. 700, a good gravel road. (You passed a trailhead at 0.3 miles for the North Trail, no. 48 in this book.) Continue 2.5 miles to a junction with the Lost Lake Road, no. 786. Turn right. Pass the Son of Middle Creek trail just beyond the turnoff. Proceed 1.3 miles to the junction of roads 786 and 719. Go right. Continue straight, past the forks at 5.3 and 8.5 miles. Park on the crest of the hill on the open summit at 9.3 miles.

The trail: Begin just below the 11,180-foot Eiseman Hut. Check your topo map: The Eiseman Hut is located just above where the jeep road switchbacks left. (Please respect hut renters' privacy.) Climb east of the hut (to its right) from your start at 11,000 feet. Search for the trail, which plays cat and mouse.

Stay east of the 11,474 point on the map. Drop at 1.2 miles, then curve around a horseshoe-shaped bowl below its ridgeline. The trail is easy to follow in this bowl. Climb a sharp rise, then leave the bowl on a steep drop. Cross a rubble field into a beautiful valley with no real trail. Now you'll regain the altitude you lost on the recent descent in a more gradual but unrelenting climb. Head northwest up this valley to the 12,000-foot lip of the crater in which Crater Lake rests.

There on the flat green crater floor pools a generous alpine lake. One senses the isolation of a rarely-seen spot in the still-untouched recesses of the Gore Wilderness. Green sweeps from the lake to the granite rim above. There, ragged ridges, pyramid peaks and dogtooth spires create a fortress wall to barricade the stunning bowl.

For some, the 12,000-foot overlook will serve as a destination. Others will want to descend to Crater Lake, 640 feet below. The trail curves northeast to the lake.

Wildflowers jam the high reaches of the Gore. In August, we spotted several varieties of gentian, including blue bottle and purple star gentian. Of the 1,100 gentian species worldwide, some 20 bloom in the Rocky Mountains. The arctic gentian, an ice-green, tubular gentian, is the author's favorite.

During World War II, Frank and Marge Haas raised pigs (fed on Camp

Hale garbage) on their 520-acre ranch on Lower Red Sandstone Road. In spring, 1950, when it snowed 40 days in a row, Marge told Frank, "Let's get out of here. This place is good for nothing but a bunch of skiers." They sold out to cattle rancher John Hanson and the ranch became Vail's base ten years later.

Ski Touring/Snowshoeing (More difficult): The 9 mile road to Eiseman Hut, used also by snowmobilers, can be fun midweek after a fresh snow on a cold day. Park at the skiers' trailhead 1.2 miles from the North Frontage Road. Skiers also reach the hut via the more challenging 6.8 mile Spraddle Creek ski route, which uses Spraddle and Middle Creek trails to reach the hut. Begin at the Spraddle Creek trailhead, just above and east of the Vail Village roundabout. Skiers and snowshoers can reserve the Eiseman Hut through the Tenth Mountain Hut and Trails System at (970) 925-5775 or www.huts.org.

Tread carefully on tundra. This delicate world supports 300 different flowers, grasses, rushes and sedges. All can survive a brutal climate, but not human trampling.

Map from TOPO! Nat'l Geographic Holdings

97

Trails near Avon, Edwards, Eagle

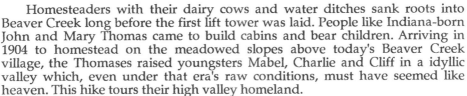

40   BEAVER LAKE

Time: 3-4 hours
Distance: 3.3 miles
Elevation gain: 1,700 feet
High point: 9,746 feet
Rating: Moderate
Usually open: June-September
Topo: Trails Illustrated, Eagle

Homesteaders with their dairy cows and water ditches sank roots into Beaver Creek long before the first lift tower was laid. People like Indiana-born John and Mary Thomas came to build cabins and bear children. Arriving in 1904 to homestead on the meadowed slopes above today's Beaver Creek village, the Thomases raised youngsters Mabel, Charlie and Cliff in a idyllic valley which, even under that era's raw conditions, must have seemed like heaven. This hike tours their high valley homeland.

Drive six miles west on I-70 from the West Vail interchange to Avon. Turn left onto Avon Road proceeding south past U.S. 6 and curve right uphill. The road name changes to Village Road and, beyond the Beaver Creek village, to Elk Track Road. The trailhead sign is 3.1 miles from I-70. After locating the trailhead, drive back to the village parking garage to leave your car.

The trail: Walk up Elk Track Road and find the path at right of the trailhead sign. Hike uphill from here through aspens to the ski mountain's upper lifts. Beaver Creek splashes over rocks below at your left. At the end of this road, you will pass under chair 11 and cross the Larkspur ski run just beyond. Now jog left, then continue ahead past the tipis and across the bridge.

During late snow years June hikers may find snow in the deep woods. Till recently a June crossing of normally-amiable Beaver Creek could be a dangerous dance across a torrent. Now a beautiful new bridge beyond the tipis preserves the joy of crossing—but blunts the adventure.

Travel south along the creek's right bank. The footpath meets an early-day wagon road. Sweet edible berries and multi-hued flowers line the path.

Walk in deep woods broken later by meadow. The valley narrows as the trail approaches Beaver Lake. The creek flows in a deep ravine below and the trail clings to a steep slope. Enter the Holy Cross Wilderness at 3 miles. The lake, beyond at 3.3 miles offers small sandy beaches, a unique feature among mountain lakes visited for this book and for the author's popular guide, *The New Summit Hiker*. The Forest Service gives this lake a good rating for brook and native trout yield. The creek earns top rating.

Ski Touring/Snowshoeing (More difficult): Both backcountry skiers and snowshoers should love the backcountry south of the ski mountain.

Use the hikers' drive directions but turn right at the Avon U.S. 6 stoplight and drive to the east parking lot (no charge). Take the free bus to Beaver Creek. Trek up the Dally run to a sign on the right indicating access to ski area out-of-boundary lodgings. Skim across Beaver Creek on a bridge at right and turn left uphill onto the road on Beaver Creek's west side. Now use the hiking directions above.

Evergreen forest gives way to open meadows. Higher up, the trail follows a wagon road, always staying close to the creek. Sometimes deep powder blankets the valley. But the contour of the road can be detected on the east slope above the creek. At a point just beyond the Holy Cross Wilderness sign at 3 miles, the trail cuts a very steep slope. For us, this slope had "avalanche" written all over it. We turned around. If a good track and very stable snow conditions exist here, you may continue to the lake just beyond.

Sample thimbleberries enroute to sand-rimmed Beaver Lake. Leave the family pooch at home--no pets except those of homeowners are allowed on Beaver Creek Village private land access.

The flowers appear on the earth, the time of singing has come, and the voice of the turtledove is heard in our land. Sg. 2:12

Time: 3 hours
Distance: 3.6 miles
Elevation gain: 788 feet
High point: 8,600 feet
Rating: Easy
Usually open: July 1-October
Topo: USGS Eagle County, Sheet 4

A sweet meander through thick aspen woods on a mulch-carpeted trail takes walkers a world away and a century back. The hike from Beaver Creek to Bachelor Gulch makes civilization fade for a bit, and the ranching lives of five eccentric "bachelors" come alive.

Drive using directions for Beaver Lake, trail no. 40.

The trail: Walk up Elk Track Road (or the Five Senses trail, left of road) to the signed Beaver Lake trailhead. Hike this footpath which later becomes road, past the water tank to find the signed Village to Village trail on the right.

Turn right, cross a bridge and enter a foliage-lined lane into a lovely aspen wood. The trail remains closed each summer until July 1 to allow the mountain's elk herd to calve and nurture their newborn young without human disruption. Hikers will find wildflowers in July, berries in August and fluttering golden aspen in September—three months to delight the senses.

Walk the bark-mulched trail. When the forest opens, hikers encounter views of the far-off Gore Range, with its rugged granite peaks. Pass the Strawberry Park lift and a few homes and later cross a paved road. After more Gore Range vistas, meet a fork in the trail. Go right. Check for traffic when crossing the paved roadways. Later, another fork gives hikers the option to visit Valley View, an overlook to Bachelor Gulch and far off across the valley to sagebrush-covered hillsides. In autumn, the aspen colonies above the sagebrush turn brilliant hues. The bluffs across the Eagle River contain sediments rich in gypsum. White gypsum seams and blobs, formed 280 million years ago when a narrow sea between the two ranges of the Ancestral Rockies evaporated, still remain visible.

The trail ends at a bridge. If Bachelor Gulch is your destination, you've arrived. Otherwise return to Beaver Creek. You can vary the route by picking up Lost Buck Spur just past the residential area near Beaver Creek Village. It descends the hillside meadow to meet the mountain road above Beaver Creek.

In sharp contrast to today's Bachelor Gulch, the haphazard collection of cabins there a century ago housed what old-timer Mamie Rodgers called "a mess of bachelors." These hard-drinking farmers, ranchers and loggers called forth suspicion from neighboring ranchers due to their offbeat behavior. Ed Howard, who was deaf, shared his cabin with his chickens, who roosted companionably on his bedstead while he dozed. John Mertz, who had lost a foot, picked a fight with a gulch resident named Holbart, who shot Mertz through his cabin door, leaving the already footless squabbler with a bone-shattered and useless wrist.

Holbart (whose first name is lost) was happily uninjured. He had a cabin mate named Archie (whose last name is lost). Their makeshift place leaked so much heat that they ate their meals wearing mittens.

When the bachelors got drunk, which happened regularly, they would stop at the store in Avon to watch the school children race their horses after class dismissal. The bachelors, normally tight with their cash, then bought the kids all they candy they wanted. "We kids didn't care how drunk they got," one recalled. "...there wasn't anything in that store that was too good for us."

Ski Touring/Snowshoeing (Moderate): Snowshoe (most popular here) or ski up the catwalk from Elk Track Road (steep but short) to the turnoff described above. Enjoy the snowy path's tranquility but stay alert to downhill skiers where the trail crosses ski runs. Also, be aware that snowboarders who stray from regular runs sometimes break out of the trees onto this trail.

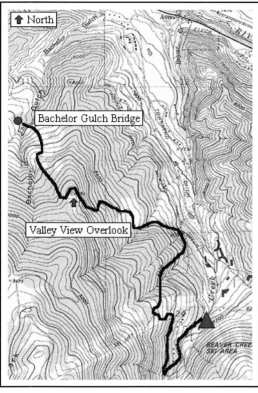

Elk herds populate the Beaver Creek woods. They nibble aspen bark in winter, creating elk "grafitti" which provides arty close-up shots for camera-toting snowshoers.
Map printed from TOPO! National Geographic Hldings (www.topo.com)

Time: 8-9 hours
Distance: 7.3 miles
Elevation gain: 3,260 feet
High point: 11,300 feet
Rating: Most difficult
Usually open: July- September
Topo: Trails Illustrated, Eagle

The Aurora Mine produced lead, silver and gold in a majestic location beside upper Turquoise Lake. While its miners exploited the rich treasures hidden in 13,670-foot Mt. Jackson's flank, ranchers below mined another natural resource: Water. This hike begins above Avon's historic homesteads along a water ditch dug by a bachelor farmer and his horse. The trail climbs to the Aurora Mine's rocky cleft.

Drive to the trailhead at Beaver Creek using directions for hike no. 40 to Beaver Lake.

The trail: Walk up Elk Track Road and use the directions for hike no. 40.

Along the wagon road you can nibble sweet red thimbleberries enroute (similar to raspberry, its broad five-point leaf has no thorn). The creek tumbles over boulders. Wildflowers, including cow parsnip, chimingbell and columbine bloom along the trail. Aspen colors the hillside at right.

Walk in deep woods broken later by meadow. The valley narrows as you approach Beaver Lake. Enter the Holy Cross Wilderness at 3 miles and reach Beaver Lake, with its pleasant sandy beaches, at 3.3 miles.

The trail continues on a densely-wooded slope high above the lake then climbs to conifer forest, a long section punctuated by fir-spiked clearings.

The trail levels out past two big meadows where flowers abound. Lower Turquoise Lake pools in this basin, a productive lake for native trout fishermen. Beyond the lake rises a massive ridge flowing from 12,799-foot Grouse Mountain at left. The West Grouse Creek Trail (this guide's hike no. 22) comes up from the northeast to terminate at Lower Turquoise Lake.

Another 20 minute walk takes you to the upper lake at 11,300 feet. Walk straight across the meadow southwest to the farthest edge of the heavy evergreen stand. Pick up the trail there. A cabin near the lake burned recently.

The walk down offers time to muse on area history. William Swift, the valley's first homesteader, arrived in Avon in 1884. The Denver & Rio Grande Railway served Avon in the 1880s. In the '90s, William H. Nottingham took advantage of U.S. homestead law. His family remained as ranchers for generations and finally sold their extensive holdings to Vail Associates for the 1978-launched Beaver Creek development. A few things happened in the intervening years: The Avon Amusement Center in 1906 hosted a grand ball that ranchers talked about for decades as "the liveliest event in the valley." And the hills came alive with Prohibition-era moonshine operations.

Ski Touring/Snowshoeing (Easy to more difficult): Check out Beaver Creek's impressive trail network at McCoy Park. Obtain special lift ticket price for skinny skiers at the chair 12 access to the high park.

Trekking the alpine runs is popular among local snowshoers.

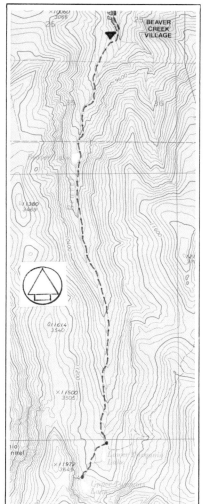

Beaver Creek flows from Turquoise Lake in rock-walled meadow. The Aurora Mine, located at the upper lake's northwest tip, penetrated the steep headwall at 11,400 feet. Two tunnels and crumbled log buildings remain.

Lower Turquoise lies in unusual flat valley. Upper lake is beyond trees, right. Backpackers can walk out an alternate route via West Grouse Creek to Minturn.

103

43   EAST LAKE CREEK

Time: 3 hours
Distance: 2 miles
Elevation gain: 800 feet
High point: 9,000 feet
Rating: Easy
Usually open: June-September
Topo: USGS Grouse Mountain, 1987

Get away from the world on a walk through aspen wood to a wide-flowing creek. This pleasant interlude affords seclusion, an experience with nature and a moderate trail that families and leisurely hikers can enjoy.

Drive I-70 west to Edwards, 10.6 miles from West Vail. Set your odometer. The trailhead is 6.4 miles from I-70. Enter the town and turn right at the stoplight. Then go 0.7 miles west on U.S. 6 to the Lake Creek Road. Turn left and proceed 1.8 miles on this road. Turn right. Now stay on the paved West Lake Creek Road and pass the Pilgrim Downs development. The paved road turns to gravel. After a tight switchback at 4WD road no. 423 climb to a newly constructed trailhead just before a road closure gate.

The trail begins in a beautiful aspen forest. If you have never taken the time to savor the scent of aspen, do so now. Touch the aspen trunk; its bark is like elephant hide. Note the constant fluttering of leaves that earns the name quaking aspen. The aspen grove is a family. Each tree is linked to another via a connector root. Groves grow uphill from a water source.

The footpath clings to a sheer slope and arcs around a concave curve. After reaching 9,000 feet the trail drops—something unusual in beginning a mountain hike—all the way to East Lake Creek.

The trail, now reconstructed for its first 5 miles, has for years diverted from routes shown on most published maps. Our route takes hikers 2 miles in to the creek, but backpackers will discover many options including Upper Camp Lake, Lake Thomas and Middle Lake. (Be aware that a beaver dam has obliterated the meadow 0.5 miles above the old mill and an avalanche has destroyed the bridge at McDonald Cabin at 8 miles.)

Joseph Brett, a French immigrant from Alsace-Lorraine, homesteaded a ranch at Lake Creek's mouth in 1878. He married the Red Cliff schoolmarm, Marie Guenon. Travelers and Ute Indians used "The Frenchman's" place as a rendezvous. But when the brutish Chief Colorow came around, Brett hid his guns and other valuables in a hole under the kitchen. The Frenchman had his feet amputated due to gangrene after falling into the icy Eagle River during the 1884 winter. When the Denver & Rio Grande arrived at Edwards in 1887, Brett set up tents to house travelers—Eagle County's first resort. Later, the town was called Berry's Ranch for homesteader Harrison Berry, then Edwards for a temporary resident, Melvin Edwards, who became Colorado Secretary of State.

Ski Touring/Snowshoeing (More difficult): The ruined Bayeta Cabins, 3.5 miles in on a snowy road, occupy a site on West Lake Creek near the mouth of Bowman Gulch. Several cabins enroute entice you to think you're there when you're not. But smashing New York Mountain views and varied terrain from meadow to fir forest satisfy as you climb the trail's 1,400-foot rise.

Start with a climb on switchbacks near the creek before two steep ascents, the first at 1 mile (if snow is thin watch rocks here.) and a second at 2 miles. A road fork at 3 miles leads left to a cabin. Stay right. Soft rolling terrain takes you past the New York Mountain trailhead to descend to the Baryeta Cabins.

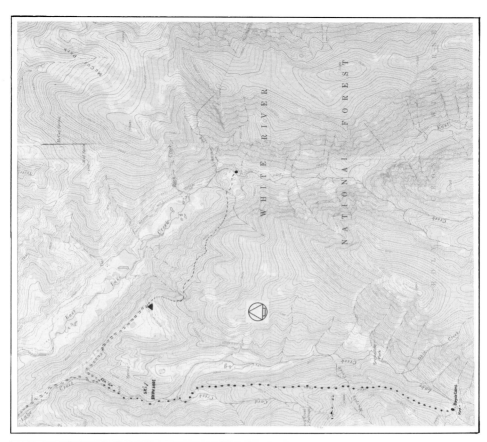

Remnants of a ranching past still linger on the way to East Lake Creek.

Time: 5 hours
Distance: 3.4 miles
Elevation gain: 1,520 feet
High point: 11,400 feet
Rating: More difficult
Usually open: July-September
Topo: USGS Fulford, Crooked Creek Pass and Mount Jackson, 1987

An intriguing ghost town named Fulford serves as a trailhead for a rewarding hike to Nolan Lake. First called Nolan's Creek Camp after an early prospector who discovered rich mines nearby in 1887, the two-part town later took the name of Arthur H. Fulford. A huge, powerful and strikingly handsome man, Fulford grew up on an early Brush Creek ranch, became town marshall for Red Cliff, then operated a rest station on the Eagle-Fulford stagecoach line. On a trek up New York Mountain to check out his mine claim on New Years Day, 1892, the amazon-like Fulford was swept to his death in an avalanche. Nolan before him had blasted out his tongue when his gun discharged while crossing Brush Creek on a slippery log—and bled to death. This trail explores the beautiful stamping grounds of these ill-starred miners.

Drive west 27 miles on I-70 from the West Vail interchange to Eagle. Take Grand Avenue to Capital and turn left. It becomes the Brush Creek/Sylvan Lake Road and now continues on paved highway 10 miles to a fork where pavement ends. Turn left onto East Brush Creek Road, no. 415 and drive 6.7 miles, continuing just past Yeoman Park Campground to the Nolan Creek Road, no. 418. Turn left and travel uphill 3.6 miles to the Nolan Creek trailhead. A road goes uphill right here leading to Upper Fulford, your trailhead. A sign at left points to Lower Fulford, road no. 419. Park at a small turnout ahead left.

The trail begins on the road uphill right. It crosses a half-bridge over rushing Nolan Creek and heads east into White Quail Gulch where Upper Fulford sprang up in 1890. Pass through the old town, which once boasted the Lamming Hotel, several boardinghouses, saloons, a livery barn, a postoffice, store and an assay office. The lower town, still alive today, had equal stature, with a schoolhouse and more miners' cabins. Nearby camps included Adelaide and New York Cabins, located on New York Mountain.

Go left at a fork past town where the road at right goes to Adelaide Park. Keep on the old mining road which later becomes a trail. At the next fork, a huge cut log marks a spot where you go right downhill for Nolan Lake.

Look for the elusive wood nymph, a small, ground-hugging plant with waxy white bloom. Enter a dark, cool forest and enjoy the boisterous flow of Nolan Creek. Meet another fork at a scree field and go uphill left here. Another confusing area occurs at a big, sloping, gray rock. It helps to know that the trail makes a big "3"-shaped turn here, going around the rock and up. A waterfall on the south valley wall, which cascades from the Nolan Lake outlet above, invites a refreshing rest stop during a steep climb. Just above lie a series of wet meadows with lush Indian paintbrush in scarlet and pink.

New York Mountain, 12,162 feet, creates a wall at left. Pass a mileage sign for New York Lake, a strenuous side trip, and continue southwest toward Nolan Lake. After two stream crossings, snake through open woods and pass a pond at left. Then travel through a small canyon and continue over rock slabs downhill to Nolan Lake.

The lake, just inside the Holy Cross Wilderness, glistens amid boulder-dotted flower meadows. Craig Peak, 11,902 feet, forms a ridge above the lake's southwest shore.

Ski Touring/Snowshoeing (Moderate): The Nolan Creek Road to old Fulford (with a possible side trip to the charming lower town) makes a refreshing ski tour or snowshoe trek. Drive the plowed road to Yeoman Park. (Call 970 328-8830 for current conditions.) Park at the Yeoman Park trailhead and climb 0.75 miles up East Brush Creek Road to the Nolan Creek Road, no. 418. The road mounts switchbacks for 3.6 miles and gains 1,120 feet in altitude. If you chose the route to Old Fulford, turn uphill right at Nolan Creek (see hiking directions) for a 0.5-mile climb to the upper town. Watch the sides of the snow-covered bridge, alert to its narrow width. The lower town, inhabited by hardy citizens through the winter, makes an interesting side trip. The lower Fulford road goes downhill left near Nolan Creek to the growing town.

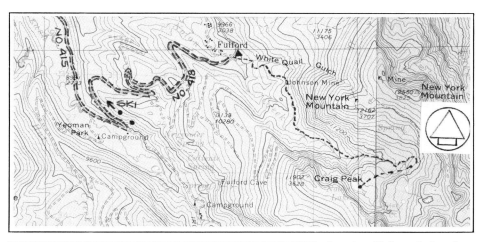

Lovely Nolan Lake has district rangers wringing their hands over resource damage. They suggest mid-week use, prohibit fire rings, request you sign in at trailhead. Hikers enter Holy Cross Wilderness near the lake. Look for rare wood nymph, white waxy bloom, in lower forest, then brilliant flower-fields near lake.

Time: 1 hour
Distance: 0.5 miles
Elevation gain: 520 feet
High point: 9,960 feet
Rating: Easy
Usually open: June-September
Topo: USGS Crooked Creek Pass, 1987

Pocketed with caves and springs, rich in gold and history, the Fulford Cave area intrigues visitors. A sometimes steep but short trail winds amid aspen to the timbered cave entrance. A nearby winter trailhead offers fun.

Drive west 27 miles from the I-70 West Vail interchange to Eagle. Take Grand Avenue west to Capital and turn left. It becomes the Brush Creek Road. Now follow this paved highway 10 miles to a fork where the pavement ends. Turn left onto the East Brush Creek Road, no. 425. At 5.7 miles on this unpaved but well-maintained road you will pass the Yeoman Park Campground. Continue another 1.4 miles to the Fulford Cave Campground. Bear left at the campground entrance to a trailhead parking area 200 feet beyond. A sign at left (north) indicates the trail to Fulford Cave.

The trail climbs the first 100 feet before winding uphill at a more gradual rate. Steep again, the path rises to a ravine then makes a sharp right. Just off the main trail to the south here is Fulford Cave Spring, one of a number of fresh-water springs nearby, including Caliente Spring and Newcomer Spring. Cross an open slope and go left at a fork to climb a few quick switchbacks before arriving at the cave entrance.

Eagle County rescue volunteers respond regularly to emergency calls from Fulford Cave. When the uninitiated enter wet, slippery, dark caves with dropoffs and other hazards, accidents occur.

The 500 mine claims in the gold-rich Fulford Mining District include a number of claims located in caves. Miners gained entrance to these nature-made tunnels by rapelling on cables from cliff-tops. In 1912, a silver strike revitalized Fulford, causing a late boom that lasted till 1918.

Another short (200 yards) trail nearby is the Yeoman Park Discovery Trail, a disabled-access trail that's great for kids. Drive into Yeoman Park Campground to the end of Loop A to locate the trail. Interpretive signs teach visitors to "sense" nature. Colorado mammals, wildflowers, rocks, trees, archaeology and water are highlighted. Squirrels, Stellar jays, gray jays and beaver in the ponds at trail's end delight young visitors.

Ski Touring/Snowshoeing (Moderate): Yeoman Park serves as the trailhead for a variety of snow tours as simple as the cruise up the Hat Creek Road to an unforgettable multi-day excursion on the Tenth Mountain Hut and Trail System. (See hike no. 46 for details on this trail network.)

We present two options for winter tours. Use driving directions shown above but continue only to Yeoman Park. Turn right and note the trailhead map. Before driving, check with the county road department, 970 328-8830.

1: Ski the gentle Hat Creek Road which rises from the Yeoman Park Campground's west boundary to a ridge where you can see the Maroon Bells. Six trails and two bridges furnish good access for ski touring. Backcountry users should skirt avalanche chutes east of Yeoman.

2: Take the 2.8 mile round trip jaunt south to the Fulford Cave Campground along the unplowed East Brush Creek Road.

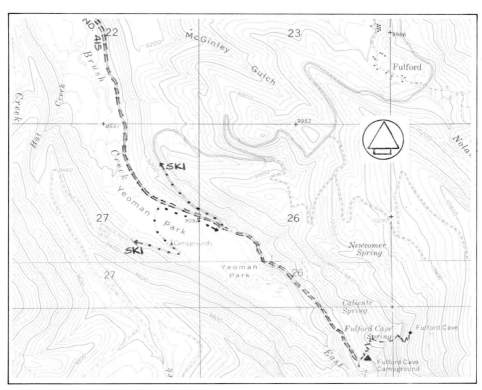

Nearby Yeoman Park serves as a trailhead for a variety of ski experiences as easy as the glide up the Hat Creek Road or as unforgettable as a multi-day excursion on the Tenth Mountain Hut and Trail System. Get more details at www.huts.org. Here, a classic ski picnic photo from the 1970s.

46   LAKE CHARLES AND MYSTIC ISLAND LAKE

Time: 6-7 hours
Distance: 6 miles
Elevation gain: 1,860 feet
High point: 11,300 feet
Rating: More difficult
Usually open: July-September
Topo: USGS Crooked Creek Pass and USGS Mt. Jackson, 1987

Stream-cut alpine flower meadows border two crystal lakes along beautiful Brush Creek—a corner of heaven. No wonder this trail is popular. While seclusion may elude hikers here, the wonder of God's creation will touch visitors to Lake Charles and Mystic Island Lake.

Drive to Eagle and then to Fulford Cave Campground using directions for hike no. 45. The trailhead is at the south end of the second parking area.

The trail begins as a road. Keep left at the first fork. The Iron Edge Trail, at right, goes to Charles Peak. (Horses are allowed on both of these trails.) Pass a large beaver pond, then climb a slope. The trail travels through a pleasant aspen wood and later penetrates deep conifer forest at about 0.3 miles. The roadbed narrows to a footpath here. As on the trail to Nolan Lake, the heavy forest retains moisture. Prepare for possible bogs and serious mud.

Stretch out your stride on the nearly-level trail here. Heavy trees curtain views but Brush Creek provides plenty of scenery, with small waterfalls and spillways common. Soon you cross the creek on a large planed log and then climb through woods to a second log crossing. The second log bridge, in disrepair at the time of this writing, may prove challenging.

This trail would rank as moderate except for two very steep sections. Soon a one-third mile ascent requires stamina. The trail passes a mammoth rock formation then becomes moderate as it travels through open meadow, forest and more meadow. Soon the second killer climb takes hikers uphill over a rough trail littered with boulders and slab rock.

The reward following that tough scramble is a stretch of small meadows thick with wildflowers. Streams cut merrily through the subalpine garden. Sometimes the creek spills over smooth slabs creating a waterslide. A quaint bridge at right crosses Brush Creek in an idyllic setting.

Large, smooth rocks bordering Lake Charles invite hikers to spread out backpack contents for lunch. Views to 12,947-foot Fools Peak and the classic cirque at valley's end add grandeur to the mountain scene. Due to heavy use, camping is allowed only in designated sites 0.5 miles from the lakes.

To continue to Mystic Island Lake, return to the main trail. The path rises along the lake's east shore then drops to a fairly level 1.4 mile footpath to Mystic at 6 miles. The trail traverses a long flower-dappled meadow with far views to the valley headwall. Wind uphill to a wide stream then turn left and walk alongside the flow as it curves right. A tarn at left marks your arrival at Mystic Island, a large alpine lake floating a dreamy isle at its southeast end. Eagle Peak soars to 13,768 feet beyond the lake.

Ski Touring (Moderate to most difficult): Yeoman Park, 1.4 miles below the hiking trailhead, offers access to the Tenth Mountain Hut and Trail System, a challenging multi-day ski touring route that links Fulford/Yeoman Park to Aspen. While most trail segments between the half-dozen huts and inns rank as intermediate, the isolated backcountry character of the route may at times require mountaineering experience and expert ski skills.

Northernmost hut on the trail is the Polar Star Inn, a lodge on the slopes of New York Mountain, 2 miles above Fulford and a tough 6.5 mile ski from Yeoman Park, with 2,000 feet in elevation gain. Skiers can also reach Polar Star from West Lake Creek above Edwards. From 4WD road 423, the tour is 7 miles via Bowman Gulch. (See driving and touring directions for hike no. 43.) Other reservation-only huts enroute to Aspen are: Peter Estin, Harry Gates, Diamond J Ranch, Margy's and McNamara Huts. Contact TMTA at (970) 925-5775.

Mystic Island Lake

Yeoman Park is a trailhead for winter trekking on the Tenth Mountain Trail System. In summer, visit Lake Charles and Mystic Island Lake mid-week or in September to avoid traffic. Hikers enter the federally-protected Holy Cross Wilderness at about 2 miles in.

Time: 6-7 hours
Distance: 5 miles
Elevation gain: 1,920 feet
High point: 11,920 feet
Rating: Moderate
Usually open: July-September
Topo: USGS Crooked Creek Pass, 1987

No trail in Eagle County can match the 360-degree views from Mount Thomas. Unsurpassed vistas to Aspen's Maroon Bells, the skyscraping Sawatch Range, the Flat Tops and the wild Gore peaks contrast with lush valleys a dizzying drop below. Because the trail straddles a ridge atop Red Table Mountain, hikers get views from the 5-mile footpath's start.

Drive west 27 miles from the I-70 West Vail interchange to Eagle. The trailhead atop Crooked Creek Pass is 21.3 miles from the Eagle exit. In Eagle take Grand Avenue west to Capital which becomes Brush Creek Road. Follow signs to Sylvan Lake. Drive 10 miles on paved road to a fork. Veer right. Pass Sylvan Lake at 16-17 miles and begin the climb up Crooked Creek Pass. Arrive at the summit about 4 miles past Sylvan Lake and drive just beyond the crest to a road on your right. (Don't take the road just before the summit.) Park here. If you have 4WD, turn right past the cattleguard and go south 0.5 miles where limited parking awaits at the trailhead.

The trail climbs on the 4WD roadbed to a wide right hairpin, then continues to a fork. Go left and follow this road to the trailhead. Look for the power line and locate the spot where the power line passes over the road. The trailhead is here, up a little sidecut to the right. The trail picks up at left.

Right away, views appear through the aspen to the rolling Frying Pan River valley, left. But wait. The Sawatch Range emerges as you switchback up a green slope above. The Elk Mountains rise to the west. The trail climbs, offering glimpses of Sylvan Lake below right (north). Watch a tricky ascent on red rubble rock with sheer valleys on each side. The dry, crumbly sedimentary rock creates *hazardous conditions* here. The red rubble rock eroded from the Maroon Formation, same as Aspen's famed Maroon Bells.

Rise to a wooded section where the flat trail winds through evergreens that could pass for a Wisconsin woods. Then emerge to a top-of-the-world timberline meadow. Cairns mark the trail as it ascends the alpine meadow.

Look ahead now for the red cirque on Mount Thomas that becomes this hike's "scenic overlook" destination. Note the ridge curve above the deep cirque. This hike follows the trail along the ridge. Then, where the continuing trail leaves the ridge to cut diagonally across to the next red-rock peak, this route climbs the green ridge cross-country to its summit.

Walk from the meadow to the ridge route, climbing on a footpath that changes from earth to rubble rock. Here where the trail abandons the ridge, leave the footpath and scramble to the summit.

Look for the Maroon Bells accented by Aspen and Ajax Mountains, southwest. Scan the Sawatch, east, and Gore Range, northeast. The long view north sweeps beyond Sylvan Lake to the gentle Eagle River valley.

This inviting valley attracted homesteader William Edwards, who claimed 156 acres at the mouth of Brush Creek in the 1880s and laid out a townsite. Eagle sprang up as a tent town, with a hotel tent, store tent, restaurant tent (venison dinner: 25 cents) and saloon tent. In 1921, Eagle took the county seat from Red Cliff, affirming the longtime farm-ranch community's future.

Ski Touring/Snowshoeing (Most difficult): Starting at Sylvan Lake, this challenging tour mounts Crooked Creek Pass, a 4-mile jaunt to a summit of expansive parks and open hillsides. (Snowshoe trekkers can climb the pass or enjoy splendid terrain around Sylvan Lake.) The unplowed road climbs from 8,600 feet at Sylvan to 10,000 at the pass. Good downhill technique will pay off on the return, where steep road and side drop-offs demand a reckoning. Do it in mid-winter or after a good snow to assure a nice base.

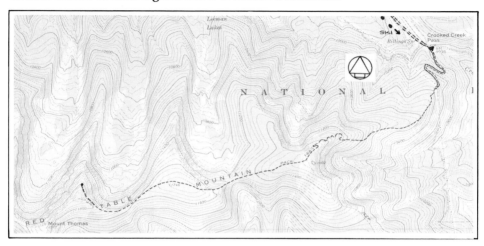

For splendid mountain views, the Mount Thomas Trail ranks number one. On a clear day, hikers can see all the way to Rocky Mountain National Park's Never Summer Range.

Ski touring on the wintry Crooked Creek Pass Road is exhilirating.

Trails above Vail

48   NORTH VAIL TRAIL

Time: 7 hours
Distance: 12 miles
Elevation gain: See sections below
High point: 9,480 feet
Rating: Easy to moderate
Usually open: June 15-October
Topo: USGS Vail West and Minturn, 1987

The North Trail is the trail of options. Hike it in sections or trek the whole trail. Drive to the trailhead or ride the bus. Mountain bike it in summer; snowshoe it in winter. Tackle it eastbound from Trappers Run for a workout or westbound from Red Sandstone for a pleasant stroll. This valley-view trail leaves it all up to you.

Birds of prey soar the skies. The Gore and Sawatch Ranges rise majestic. Aspen mixes with pine. The south-facing trail delivers a long season.

The Town of Vail teamed up with the Forest Service and a community volunteer corps in 1996 to create an eventual 12-mile trail on the north slope above Vail. The Middle Creek section debuted in summer, 2001. Access is a key advantage. Trailhead bus stops benefit visitors, older kids and hikers exiting at trailheads different from their start. Wildlife protection closes the trail from April 15 till June 15.

Several trailheads tap into the new trail. They are (west to east) Trappers Run in West Vail; Buffehr Creek Road; Red Sandstone Road; and Middle Creek, which uses the Spraddle Creek trailhead as its east terminus. You can hike this trail in various segments:

1. Trappers Run to Buffehr Creek.

Distance: 5.5 miles	**Elevation gain:** 1,520 feet
Rating: Moderate	**High point:** 9,200 feet

Drive or ride the bus and walk to the corner of North Frontage Road West and Arosa Drive just west of I-70 West Vail exit 173. Parking is available.

The trail begins in cool fir and aspen, a refreshing start for a zip to the Davos dirt road. It connects you after 0.4 miles with a single track trail, just 100 feet from another trail-access street above called Cortina Lane. (If you get on board there you eliminate 1 mile and 441 elevation feet of metabolism-boosting effort. But you'll need a drop-off because there is no parking at Cortina Lane.) Now climb (680 feet, 0.7 miles) on a ravine-circling route through mixed aspen forest to the ridgeline.

One reward at ridgetop is the Mount of the Holy Cross with its 1,500 foot granite cross crowning the magnificent Sawatch Range southwest. Another is hawk and golden eagle sweeping the sky to hunt. (Look for raptor nests.)

Hikers pop out of trees on a fairly level route to view a dramatic rock formation, then a panorama of Vail, Beaver Creek, Sawatch (Notch, Whitney) and Gore (Uneva, Zodiac Spires) peaks. After dense forest comes Antenna point, another vista spot, before the descent to Buffehr. Exit the trail by veering right to access the switchbacks leading down to the Buffehr road.

Hikers have gained a total of 1,520 feet altitude. By reversing this hike, beginning at the Buffehr Creek access, you can eliminate about one-third of the altitude gain, reducing it to a more moderate hike gaining 1,040 feet.

2. Buffehr Creek to Red Sandstone.

Distance: 3 miles   **Elevation gain:** 870 feet
Rating: Easy   **High Point:** 9,000 feet

Drive I-70 to West Vail exit 173 and go 0.7 miles east on the North Frontage Road to Buffehr Creek Road. Turn left; go 0.2 miles to the trailhead.

The trail heads south, which looks wrong but is not, and switchbacks for 0.8 miles. Go right at two forks to meet the main trail. Pass an active beaver pond and traverse 1992/2004 avalanche debris (*winter users: Caution!*). Then negotiate a possibly tricky Buffehr Creek crossing at 8,400 feet. Hikers ascend through trees to reach the ridge and 9,000 feet altitude. Now an easy walk yields great views. No streams flow so bring water if your pooch is along (leash required). Tote water for yourself too because this ridge can get hot! Soon switchbacks ease the drop to Red Sandstone.

3. Red Sandstone to Middle Creek.

Distance: 3.5 miles   **Elevation gain:** 1,120 feet
Rating: Moderate   **High point:** 9,480 feet

Drive from I-70 Vail exit 176 (or the Vail roundabout) 1 mile west along the North Frontage Road to Red Sandstone Road. Turn right and proceed 0.4 miles to a trailhead at left.

The trail ascends due north along Red Sandstone Road to a gate and Fire Hazard sign. Turn east and climb the gulch in dense aspen-fir to break out at some rocky outcroppings. The North Trail's highest views are here. Drink in the ridgetop panorama, then meet the Son of Middle Creek Trail. Go right. Old sheepherding signs may remain here. (Vail, less suitable for cattle, flourished with sheep-raising.) Get ready for a drop south to trail's end at the Middle-Spraddle Creek trailhead above I-70, a short hop from Vail Village.

Ski Touring/Snowshoeing (Moderate): Stay warm on a south slope but expect a short season. Seclusion in snow-mantled pines gives way to sun-bathed ridge vistas. This wonderful variety means trail conditions may vary early and late season, with snow changing from powder to hardpack or slush.

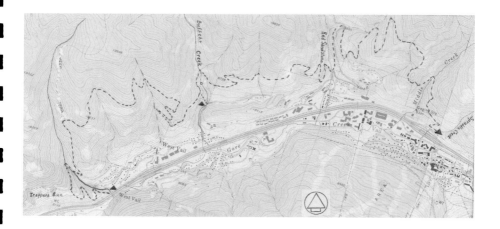

Time: 5-6 hours
Distance: 4 miles
Elevation gain: 2,000 feet
High point: 10,080 feet
Rating: More difficult
Usually open: June 16-October (closed April 15-June 15)
Topo: Trails Illustrated Vail, Frisco, Dillon

A sheer ridgetop gives hikers a big crescent view of the wilderness Piney Lakes region, the rich Red Sandstone area and Vail Mountain, ribboned by ski trails. Along the way to this destination ridge, hikers on the Buffehr Creek Trail encounter an intriguing mix of ecosystems, including sun baked slopes and murky pine forest, plus an ethereal aspen woods straight out of another world.

Drive the North Frontage Road east from the West Vail roundabout 0.7 miles to Buffehr Creek Road. Turn left and proceed 0.2 miles to a trailhead on the left. If parking is full, continue to additional parking ahead right. This is one of several trailheads for the North Trail, which links into the Buffehr Creek Trail. A map board here gives hikers a clear picture of the North Trail system.

The trail crosses a bridge over Buffehr Creek and switchbacks up a dry, brushy hillside. Look for miners candle, mules ear and scarlet gilia in June and raspberries in August. At the fork where a wide path continues straight ahead, a narrow path veers right. Go right. Soon you'll cross the creek.

A stiff climb brings you to a pretty aspen glade where impressive Vail Village and Vail Mountain views compensate for the ascent. Later, a signed fork indicates that the North Trail goes right across the hillside. The Buffehr Creek route, your trail, goes left uphill.

When you finally conquer the initial steep slope, you'll step into a mature aspen forest where hundred of huge trunks rise from a green forest floor. If you expect to glimpse elves here, you're not alone. The woods resonate a mystical aura. The mottled trunks, etched by elk graffiti (caused by elk nibbling the bark), look as if inscribed by fairy writing.

Wild rose, columbine, delphinium and thistle color the forest floor. The only drawback here is trail damage caused by mountain bike use. In some cases, the trail forms a V-shape difficult for hikers to walk on.

Contrast the rich aspen forest with the dense pine ahead. Trees create a canopy, dim as a tunnel. Deeper and deeper into the pines you go, and darker and darker the forest becomes. Plant life dwindles to kinnikinnick groundcover and yellow-flowering heart-leaf arnica, which love acid pine soil and dim light.

Later the trail joins a road, crossing a power line cut with views to the Gore and Sawatch Ranges. The Gore bears the name of an Irish baronet-huntsman. The Sawatch runs for 100 miles south of Vail and contains 15 peaks over 14,000 feet, including Colorado's highest, Mount Elbert at 14,417 feet.

Cross a new-growth lodgepole "nursery," then mount Panorama Ridge, this hike's destination. Jumbled Eagles Nest Wilderness peaks shelter the Piney Lake drainage at left (north). Alpine lakes and waterfalls (see trails 36-38) await hikers there. Red Sandstone Road, an access to wilderness hiking trails and a mountain bikers' mecca, stretches below (east). Vail Village nestles in a former sheep ranching valley and Vail Mountain spreads its slopes at right (south).

The ridge makes a nice picnic stop before the return to the trailhead. Hikers who want a one-way trip can leave a second car at the Red & White

Mountain Road's junction with the Buffehr Creek Trail, 1.6 miles ahead.

The Vail valley, originally known as the Gore valley, housed 27,000 sheep in 1959 but only four year-round landowners. Newell Buffehr was one of the hardy quartet. Today his ranch today provides access to several hiking routes and a protected retreat for luxury homes.

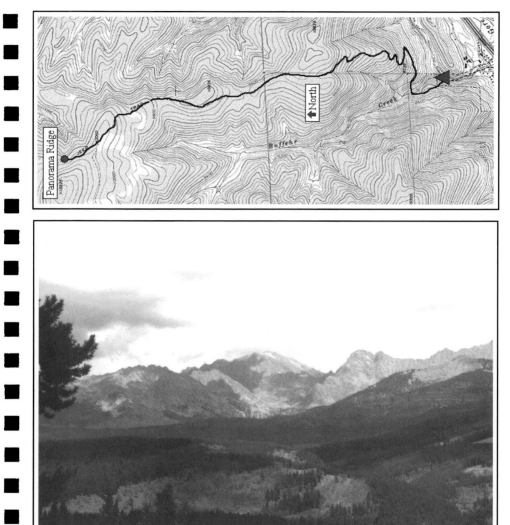

The Buffher Creek Trail to Panorama Ridge affords prime views. Hikers begin on a dry slope. Look for potentilla there. Legend says that its leaves, placed in Ute Indian moccasins, prevented hiking blisters. Map printed from TOPO! National Geographic Holdings (www.topo.com)

Time: **2-3 hours**
Distance: **4.6 miles**
Elevation loss: **2,270 feet**
High point: **10,350 feet**
Rating: **Easy**
Usually open: **June-October**

A Colorado mountain strawberry comes in a small package. But its strawberry flavor is intense—piercing and sweet. You'll like this trail's strawberries, gooseberries and thimbleberries. These look like raspberries but have a broad five-point leaf and no thorn. Even without the berries, you will savor this lush downhill hike through flower meadows, thick aspen and alongside splashing streams.

Drive the South Frontage Road to the Lionshead gondola parking structure, just west of the main Vail village. Park and walk to the gondola building. Pick up a trail map here.

The lift runs daily from 10 a.m.-4:30 p.m. (and till 10 p.m. Thursday-Saturday) from late June through Labor Day, with weekend service into October when the weather holds. (Call 970 476-9090 for information.) The gondola whisks you up 2,270 feet from base to Eagle's Nest, providing views to the primitive Gore Range/Eagle's Nest Wilderness to the north. Creek drainages from west to east are Red Sandstone Creek (across the valley), Booth, Pitkin, Bighorn and Gore Creeks. See *The Vail Hiker's* first section for these trails.)

The trail begins to the left as you exit the gondola. Starting on the same path as Fireweed, the route up to the Wildwood Shelter, hikers walk east to a junction, then begin the downhill drop on the Berrypicker Trail. Crossing ski trails including Lodgepole, Ledges, Minnie's Mile and Born Free, the footpath follows several wide switchbacks in and out of woods. In the trees look for birds such as western tanager, evening grosbeak, ruby-throated hummingbird, red-shafted flicker, the gray Canadian jay and the bright blue stellar jay.

One of the ski runs you cross is International where giant slalom races are held. Look for columbine, wild rose and sweetpea nearby.

Before Vail Mountain's 1962 debut as a ski area (Lionshead came a few years later), the meadowed slopes and green valley were covered by sheep. Early day homestead ranchers spread in 160-acre parcels along Gore Creek. Ranch families included the Katsos, Baldaufs, Shivelys and the Greek rancher, Gus Kiahtipes, whose summer cabin is now a bus shelter in East Vail.

Ski Touring (Easy): The Vail Nordic and Nature Center offers 15 kilometers of groomed track free to cross-country skiers. Its Center building, near the Vail Golf Clubhouse, serves as a warming hut daily from 9 a.m.-4 p.m., serving snacks and drinks. Nordic ski lessons are available through the Vail/Beaver Creek Cross-country Ski School.

Drive the south frontage road to Vail Valley Drive turning at the Vail Golf Course sign. Free parking is available at the clubhouse. Or, take the free public bus. Since many municipalities prohibit golf course skiing, please observe all track rules to preserve golf course skier privileges: No dogs are allowed on these trails. Joggers and walkers are prohibited. Faster skiers have the right of way. No littering is allowed. Now, have fun! Views to the sky-piercing Gore Range and snow-crusted Gore Creek add to the joy of skiing here.

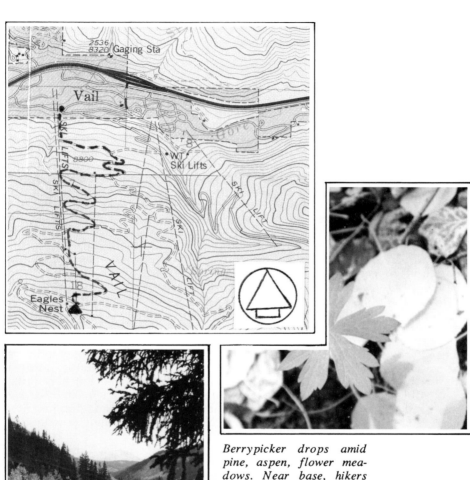

Berrypicker drops amid pine, aspen, flower meadows. Near base, hikers can branch to Vail or Lionshead. Look for huckleberries at fork.

APPENDIX: THE COMMANDO RUN

Called "Colorado's most superb ski tour," the Commando Run is also known as the "18-mile Run" and the "Vail Pass to Vail" tour.

Drive: Leave a car in Vail. Drive I-70 to the Vail Pass summit and park.

The trail begins on the Shrine Pass Road, just west of the interchange. Ski and snowmobile use has been separated here. Ski the Shrine Pass Road snowmobile track (or follow the signed cross-country ski route to Shrine Mountain Inn, then pick up the road). The road switchbacks north, then southwest before heading west and later north-northwest. Follow an easy uphill grade almost 2 miles to a flat area with good Gore Range views. This is an indication that you are approaching the indistinct 11,050-foot Shrine Pass summit at 2.3 miles. A sign here reads "Entering White River National Forest."

Descend to the Shrine Mountain Inn, a Tenth Mountain Trail ski hut, and beyond it the marked Holy Cross overlook at 3.75 miles. Drop to the Timber Creek Road at just past 4 miles. Turn right and climb for 0.5 miles to go left at an intersection with the Lime Creek Road. The hiking trail is on the right here just 0.1 miles past the intersection. Most skiers continue past this to a clearing where a hillside to the right displays scattered trees. This is the southeast flank of Pt. 11,611'; climb it, eventually on switchbacks, to pass just 200 feet below its summit. Progress beyond the clearing to enter the woods and climb. Contour around the peak's south-facing slope. At this point, you emerge onto a forested ridgeline at about 6 miles. Ski west along the ridgetop for 0.5 miles, then climb to the open snowfields of Pt. 11,710'. Here you confront magnificent Gore Range views east and north, along with the Mount of the Holy Cross and Notch Mountain among the wild Sawatch Range peaks southwest. The Tenmile and Mosquito Ranges dominate views southeast and south.

The clearings on Pt. 11,710' run northwest. Ski to the end of the clearings and note that the ridge veers northeast.

Curve north-northeast above the steep drop of Timber Creek bowl and meet a grove of huge Englemann spruce at about 7.2 miles. Keeping left of the ridgetop, drop through powder to a wooded saddle. Continue northeast across this saddle toward Pt. 11,618'. Avoid straying too far left here (hikers make the same mistake). Stay close to the ridge crest and then climb the west side of Pt. 11,618', bypassing the actual summit. Rejoin the ridgetop just north of the summit. Ski along the wooded ridge, then drop on rolling powder fields to the open saddle of Two Elk Pass at 8.8 miles.

Begin the climb up steep, treeless 11,816-foot Siberia Peak (marked "Red" on topo), the highest point on the tour and the place to watch most for avalanche danger. Test the snowpack for stability and do not proceed if avalanche conditions exist. The eastern edge (far right) of this slope terminates in a cliff that builds dangerous cornices. Stay well away. Switchback up the east slope, crossing about 50 feet below the summit on the west side. Enjoy views of Vail's China and Sunup bowls (west).

Descend north along a broad ridge, following a line of clearings. Enter the trees at about 10.3 miles. You will travel north on a logging road to the first road switchback. Here turn left (west) down the fall line and plunge through powder in Mushroom Bowl. (Go north for an easier descent.) Near the bottom of the bowl, keep north toward the right side of the drainage to locate the Mill Creek Road. Follow the snowy roadbed for 3.3 miles to the Golden Peak lift of the Vail Ski Area. Then ski down a maintenance road or climb Golden peak and ski alpine runs to the base.

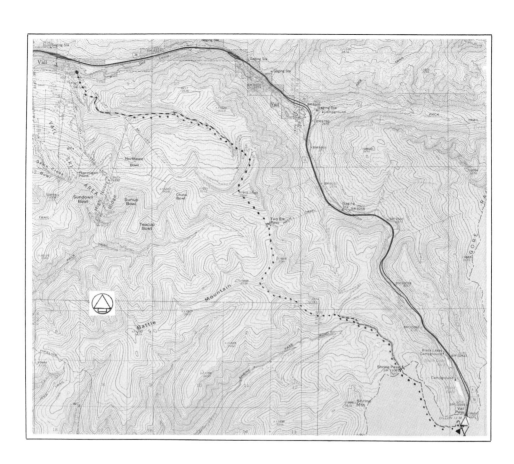

Artist Thomas Moran painted this Mount of the Holy Cross scene from East Cross Creek. He struggled over wet, slippery boulders and deadfall so heavy that pack animals could not hazard the route. He arrived exhausted at this much-hailed scene.

50 Scenic Trails

Give THE VAIL HIKER to a Friend

Friends, family members, co-workers--anyone who loves the mountain outdoors--will delight in discovering Vail and Eagle County with THE VAIL HIKER and Ski Touring Guide. This "gift that keeps on giving" features a variety of alpine locales from tranquil to breathtaking. No other trail guide can match THE VAIL HIKER's specific, comprehensive and accurate coverage of Eagle County hiking and ski trails.

Just tear out this page, then complete and mail the order blank below. The author will write a special inscription for your friend if you indicate his or her name below (last line).

Please mail THE VAIL HIKER to this address:

Name _____

Address _____

City _____ State _____ Zip _____

THE VAIL HIKER	17.95
Postage:	2.50
Sales Tax: (Colorado only)	.54

Checks or Money Orders Only

Total Enclosed: $ 20.99

Send to: Alpenrose Press
Box 499
Silverthorne, CO 80498
(970)468-6273
www.alpenrosepress.com

Please autograph my copy: _____
Your friend's name

ORDER SUMMIT COUNTY BOOKS TODAY -- POSTAGE FREE

SUMMIT

Mary Ellen Gilliland's lively history of Summit County's colorful gold and silver rush days.

Crazy characters... whispering ghost towns... nomadic Ute Indians... narrow-gauge railways... bawdy mine camps... The whole colorful history of Colorado's skyscraping Summit County... 348 pages... more than 100 antique photographs... a lively, well-written and popular gold rush history.

SUMMIT	18.95
Postage:	2.50
Sales Tax: (Colorado only)	.55

Checks or Money Orders Only

Total Enclosed: $22.00

Send to: Alpenrose Press
            Box 499
            Silverthorne, CO 80498
            (970)468-6273
            www.alpenrosepress.com

VISIT THE GHOST TOWNS with *BRECKENRIDGE!*

BRECKENRIDGE!

Explore famous gold mines... discover ghost towns... tour a gem historic district.

15 ghost towns and sites

    12 major mines

        2 gold dredges

            43 historic buildings

                Jeep and auto tours, self-guided walking tours, ski jaunts

BRECKENRIDGE	4.95
Postage:	1.50
Sales Tax: (Colorado only)	.30

Checks or Money Orders Only

Total Enclosed: $ ____

Send to: Alpenrose Press
                Box 499
                Silverthorne, CO 80498
                (970)468-6273
                1 (800) 579-1179 (Orders only)